THE CHARTER OF THE WORLD UNION

The responsibility of every nation is for the entire world and
The responsibility of the world is for every nation of the world entire.

"The World Union" is- by the nations, of the nations, and for the nations &
"Every nation's responsibility is for the entire world and the world's responsibility is for every nation of the world entire."
And thus, it will be the savior, servant and master of supreme stature of the entire world.

R.N.MOHAN

2016

1

Dedicated to
All the leaders of the world
In particular
Barack H Obama/ Donald Trumph
Vladimir Putin
David Cameron/Theresa May
Presidents/Prime Ministers of
Brazil, India, South Africa
China
Who are all ardently aspiring for the world welfare besides
The Peace, Progress and prosperity of the world entire.

Published By Createspace

Book Designed By, jacket Designed by, Jacket Illustration by Createspace

Library of Congress Cataloging-Publication Data
R.N.MohanCreatespace, USA
The Charter of the World Union

ISBN xxx-x-xxx-xxxxx-x

Manufactured in USA

Unite, all nations of the world
Unite, the whole humanity of the world

Contents

Prologue

I. Introduction

II. The Existing International Organizations
(For concerned regional economic cooperation, the emergence of the World Union)

III. United World Educational Organization (UWEO)
(For global educational promotion and cooperation)

IV. The Jury of the World
(For resolving all global conflicts and confrontations)

V. The Universal Code of Conduct
(For global acceptance and practice by all nations and all nationals)

VI. Some Existing Intercontinental Organizations and their Associated countries
(For concerned regional countries' economic cooperation and sustainable development)

VII. The World Union's Continental and Sub-continental and Regional Unions
(For the concerned areas' growth and development; peace, progress and prosperity)

VIII. The World Union
(For Universal solidarity and brotherhood, and for the development of the world entire, The Road map of formation of the Union)

IX. The Nations
(For unity and solidarity of all nations and their advancement with amity and friendship)

X. The World Trade, Business and Commerce
(For global trade and the globalization with mutual cooperation of all nations)

XI. The Charter of the World Union
(The universal constitution with universal code of conduct)

XII. Conclusion

Epilogue

Prologue

I discussed about "*The World Union*" as the final turning point and as the destiny-manifest of the world in my earlier book entitled, "The Turning Points." Buddha and Jesus Christ were contemporaries, and both stood for world peace and propounded the same and thus, became the saviors of the world. Now in the world, for the phenomenon that the whole world is to be molded to be one, the time exactly ripened. The path of progress and prosperity through united world system has been laid. Nay, the foundation for the "The World Union" has been laid.

Gone were days of conflicts and confrontations for power by the expansion of their empires or for enforcing some ideology, because of people became more knowledgeable with vision and concept of life. To possess knowledge is great, but to have wisdom is supreme and to be enlightened is supremely great. Now in the busy schedule of man's life, instead of thinking and arguing about this concept or that concept, adjust and assimilate every concept and move on amicably with all and thus, a person in the modern society goes to a Hindu temple, Christian Church and Mohammadan Masjid or a Sikh Gurudwara with an equal pace of respect and enlightenment. But as an exception the ideological differences in some pockets of the world alone rising disturbances, which are not at all impediments for the unity of the world. It is going on. The world is in its transition and hence the change is imminent. The whole world is shrinking into a miniature world and all the humanity coming closer and closer, forgetting all sorts of differences and learning to live together in congenial, serene and tranquil milieu. The ideal of human unity is going to be fulfilled.

Consequently, the need aroused for some *common code of conduct* that is *the universal code of conduct,* instead of any religion, ideology or faith as they result in sectarian attitudes. Inherently, it entered into process the world over. That universal code of conduct for the individuals and for the nations is in the offing, in the one world system and that has been well-addressed in this tiny volume.

R. N. Mohan

I. Introduction

I am advocating the peace, progress and prosperity of the world by uniting the whole world through the formation of 'the World Union' as mentioned earlier and will be well dealt with in these following pages.

There are some people who are ardently struggling and striving for the world development and the world peace, which is praiseworthy and highly applauded the world over (e.g. the recent U.S-Cuba détente and so many others like Trans Pacific Partnership Deal etc., by the American Government). The Syrian problem has to be solved amicably by negotiations and any other future world calamities are to be averted peacefully.

During 1483-1546 AD Francisco de Vitoria[6], conceived the concept of "The Republic of the whole world." Especially, in the recent past the American President Barack Obama's speech in Cairo was the good step for building the bridge of peace between the East and the West. In very recent times, in the present twenty first century, after two years of dialogues together with international partners, United States had achieved the nuclear deal with Iran, with which eras of acrimony is over. And the American Nuclear Arms Control Treaty with Russia is remarkable. These are all broad and enduring deals that will positively prevent any country from obtaining nuclear weapons. These transactions indicate the real, meaningful and purposeful revolution, their leadership and diplomacy can bring the transformation that makes besides USA, the entire world safe, secure and prosperous. Other good examples are the recent meetings of the American President Barack Obama with Chinese Premier Jinping, Indian Premier Narendra Modi, and Pakistan Premier Nawaz Sharif. And this Union will lead the world towards pleasant and peaceful world minimizing all sorts of differences and conflicts between countries and between ideologies.

The foundations for "*The World Union*," have already been laid and now its emergence is at stones through away distance. Primarily, in United Nations Organization, there is a flaw-how many nations are to be united. Not necessarily all (out of 238 only 196 UN member-states). Changing the UNO is the ardent desire of all the people and all the leaders the world over and the same was echoed in the recent General Assembly of UNO even. (And another example is the recent G4 Summit on changes in UNO and also G20 summit for world peace). And hence, is this- "*The World Union*." This will comprise mandatorily, the membership of all nations of the world. Then all nations work united for the development of the entire world including their individual nations with "*Universal Solidarity and brotherhood with Mutual Cooperation and Co-ordination.*" It is a distinct destiny for that Union unlike UNO's, rectifying its defects.

Even in the ancient times the idea of conquering the whole world was there in the minds of some people like Genghis Khan, Alexander the Great, of late Napoleon Bonaparte, Adolf Hitler and so on who thought of becoming the world conquerors.

That concept was survived in the middle ages as well. In the later ages the concept changed to the world government that was in the air. It was during 1483-1546 AD Francisco de Vitoria[6], conceived the concept of "The Republic of the whole world." He was the founder of International Law. In 1625 Hugo Grotius[12] wrote a book entitled "On the Law of War and Peace," which is being considered as the foundation for international law. In 1795 Immanuel Kant[vii] stated that the world citizenship is needed for establishing world peace in his article "the Perpetual Peace."

It was in nineteenth century Joseph Smith[13] propounded 'Theo democracy' and his council to rule as a World Government leading to the Kingdom of God. And in 1811 AD a German philosopher Karl Krause (1781-1832 AD), in his article entitled, "Archetype of Humanity" suggested the five continents namely Europe, Asia, Africa, America and Australia were to be the five states of World Republic.

Alfred Lord Tennyson[viii], an English Poet in 1842 AD in his poem ,"Locksley Hall," mentioned about "*universal law*" and "*the parliament of man, the federation of the world.*"

In the second half of the nineteenth century Bahá'u'lláh[i, ii] pronounced his united world concept saying: "The earth is but one country and mankind its citizens".

Ulysses S. Grant commented, "I believe at some future day, the nations of the earth will agree on some sort of congress, which will take cognizance of international questions of conflicts and whose decisions will be as binding as the decisions of the Supreme Court are upon us".

Harry Truman U.S. President in 1940s commented that "We must make the United Nations continue to work, and to be a going concern, to see that difficulties between nations may be settled just as we settle difficulties between states here in the United States. When Kansas and Colorado fall out over the waters in the Arkansas River, they don't go to war over it; they go to the Supreme Court of the United States, and the matter is settled in a just and honorable way. There is no difficulty in the whole world in settling the problems in exactly the same way in a world court".

Garry Davis of France propounded for the World Government in UN Assembly and commenced the organization.

Numerous international organizations came into their being promoting global unity and binding the nations of the world. For example Universal Postal Union, International Telegraphic Union, World Health Organization, Interpol, World Trade Organization, International Chamber of Commerce and so on.

League of Nations attempted for the unity of the world but failed. Some other attempts were being made by Worldwide Communistic Society, Nazi Germany under Hitler. Some vain attempts were also being made by the Atlantic Charter at the behest of Winston Churchill, but that lead to the formation of United Nations, which is partially successful besides many failures. The things were transforming in the world scenario rapidly.

There are numerous regional and continental and intercontinental organizations as well, which are aspiring continental and regional integration and development. Some of them are: African Union (AU), Arab League or Arab Union, Association of Southeast Asian Nations (ASEAN), Caribbean Community (CARICOM) or Caribbean Federation, Central American Integration System (SICA), Commonwealth of Independent States (CIS), Commonwealth of Nations, Cooperation Council for the Arab States of the Gulf (CCASG), Eurasian Economic Community (EurAsEC), Warsaw Pact, Organization of American States (OAS), South Asian Association for Regional Cooperation (SAARC), BRICS, Turkic Council (TurkKon), Union of North American Nations (UNASUR), Union of Australia and New Zealand, North American Free Trade Agreement (NAFTA) or North American Union, Pacific Islands Forum or Pacific Union, Eurasian Union, European Union, North Atlantic Treaty Organization (NATO), Shanghai Cooperation Organization, Organization of Islamic Cooperation, Proposed United Nations Parliamentary Assembly and so on, and all about them will be discussed in the next chapter.

But in fact all along these centuries, the full-fledged and the needed world body couldn't take appropriate shape. Now the time has ripened. Efforts are needed to establish "the World Union" comprising of all nations of the world superseding all the above unions, organizations including UNO, and have to work for the advancement of the world in all possible dimensions economic, social, political and religious.

This 'World Union' will bring the contemplations of these unions into practical reality.

II. The Existing International Organizations

(For concerned regional economic cooperation)

On January 8, 1918, it was Woodrow Wilson, who presented his peace proposal to the Congress for establishing just and everlasting peace all over the world, *and to prevent all future wars and all conflicts would be settled peacefully through treaties and negotiations*. His blueprint for peace known as the "Fourteen Points" was studied by the people around the world, which dealt with freedom-economic and political of all nations in the world and especially the fourteenth point stressed the need of an international association of the countries of the world called "The League of Nations," which was a crucial element of the peace efforts to prevent any future world war to happen again. The peace conference at Versailles palace outside Paris in 1919 was a biggest turning point for the world history itself. On January 28, 1919 itself, the Treaty of Versailles was signed. Perhaps this was the first international organization for the peace move the world over. Just after two decades there were further moves for world peace.

It was during 1941 Franklin D. Roosevelt furthered the idea of League of Nations and promoted the idea of United Nations instead of the earlier. Later the allied powers namely USSR, USA, and Great Britain, which were the big three, which Franklin called 'United Nations' joined and planned for permanent peace in the world. Franklin Roosevelt was the first American President to have diplomatic ties with USSR. He said that his dream of ever-lasting peace on the face of earth will become into reality through 'United Nations Organization.'

In 1945 Franklin D. Roosevelt participated in the Yalta Conference, the most important turning point of convergence, with Winston Churchill and Joseph Stalin and their deliberations were about post-war strategies and formation of a more powerful organization of all willing nations of the world interested in creation of war free world. This was the most important second move in the history of the world.

And during 1000-2000 AD many parts of the world faced territorial conflicts and consequently, numerous wars held and religious and ideological differences affected the peace and stability of the different countries of the world.

Also this global warfare heralded Nuclear Age by the usage of the nuclear weaponry in the wars the world over. This was highly devastating, and that led to mass destruction in moments resulting high human loss. By 1942 Germany and Japan become isolated, besieged and defeated by the allied powers. By the end of the World War II discussions on the postwar peace was on the air. People all over the globe vexed of wars and wished to have peace to prevail. Then in the meeting of the "Big Three" the allied leaders namely- Joseph Stalin of Russia, Winston Churchill of Britain and Franklin D. Roosevelt of USA met at Yalta in February 1945 made fruitful deliberations about the postwar strategies and about the highly weakened the Nazi Empire of Germany as Germany was totally responsible for the World War II.

The whole world politics took a new turn with two different concepts of democratic capitalism of USA and the communism of USSR, and each tried to dominate the other. And that led to the manifestation of "Cold War" resulting in the Korean War, Cuban Missile Conflict, which might have led to global warfare again at the behest of America and Russia, Vietnam War and many other conflicts as well. That further led to building up nuclear weapons of mass destruction on both sides, and then if at all any other world war broke out nothing remains on the face of the earth.

The economic and military strength of USA made it a global super power and with the aid of USA, Japan emerged as one of the richest countries in the world, developing in all possible aspects like industry and technology.

Simultaneously, Peoples Republic of China was started blooming to become another world super power to rival USSR, whereas USA intervened in Korea and Vietnam to countermand the communism. Subsequently, the collapse of Soviet System in 1989-91 ended the cold war between America and Russia saving the world from all wars. It as in 1949 North Atlantic Treaty Organization (NATO) was established under its canopy, the Unites States provided guarantee of security to the Western Europe. In its turn the USSR and its allied countries in the Eastern Europe formed the Warsaw Pact to provide security to the countries of the Eastern Europe. Thus, literally the Europe was divided into two zones the Eastern Europe and the Western Europe. When the "Cold War" ended between USSR and USA their rivalry also simultaneously ended. After the collapse of USSR, USA maintained its world economic dominance. Then open economy, free market trade, globalization were leading ahead to form a new world system. Under the canopy of European Union, the Western Europe is also progressing well economically with political unity and economic stability.

But unluckily the Eastern Europe under the grip of Soviet Union is still under pressure of Communism and with strained economic stability.

Germany was reunited in 1990 by demolishing the Berlin Wall, which was a great move for peace and tranquility in Germany rectifying its earlier defects and misdeeds.

But only in the Middle East accompanied by the rise of Islam, instability is reigning supreme in the countries particularly Syria, Egypt, Saudi Arabia, Iran, Iraq, Afghanistan, Kuwait, Lebanon, Palestine and Pakistan.

But tremendous efforts were being made around the globe to establish "Peace" all over the world and for uniting the world by all means like economic, political and social as well.

While the world is developing with growth and innovations in one way the other way some sort of ideological differences crept in, into the realms of the world society consequently, some conflicts arose like "war on terrorism," which was alive for a short time.

In the recent past the globalization had had its tremendous impact in almost all countries in the whole world in all aspects like political, social and economic besides willing reformations and vehement resistance. The territorial boundaries are constrained to change, economic status modified and human living style improved.

In the global perspective the political, cultural, social, economic and religious aspects concerned to the world's human society are going to change in numerous ways, facing enumerable turning points in their development namely-renaissance, enlightenment from the days of dark and times of superstition. For example, the highly liberalized economies of South Korea, Taiwan, and Singapore spectacularly developed technologically and industrially.

By the end of twentieth century and by the beginning of twenty-first century, the world economy shaped into global businesses. The World Trade Organization was established in 1995. The globalization is rapidly growing around the world by the expansion of transportation, telecommunication and the other advanced and sophisticated technologies like internet, world web, and networking.

The most magnificent aspects that are occurring, which are bringing unity and solidarity amongst nations and continents with mutual understanding for mutual cooperation and coordination for overall development and growth as well instead of waging war or invasions-the formation of the world bodies. How continents are coming closure, and how the nations in a continent are coming together and uniting, as mentioned earlier, can be seen in the following lines.

1. North American Union is in the offing primly with membership of USA, Mexico and Canada, which will be on the similar lines of European Union, with common currency called Amero, which will be the union of the countries of North American continent with possible extension to further Central America and South America as well. It will work for the union and mutual cooperation and mutual development in all aspects like political, social, economic and cultural with eased international trade practices and collective industrialization measures.

2. Union of South American Nations UNASUR is a regional union with its members namely- Bolivia, Columbia, Ecuador, Peru, Argentina, Brazil, Paraguay, Uruguay, Venezuela, Chile, Guyana, and Suriname with prime objectives of economic development, free trade practices, defense strategies, and thus, uniting nations and people of the region. The other territories namely-Easter Islands, Sa Adres Y Providencia, Isla Aves, Argentine and Chilean Antarctic bases are also members of the union.

3. The **G-20** is the group of countries, which are highly industrialized and the leading economies of the world namely USA, UK, France, Germany and Japan came together called the Group 5 or the G-5 countries and they meet in annual summits and discuss matters of global concern. Such groupings have been formed namely G-5, G-6, G-7, and the latest is the G-20, which comprises the membership of latest emerging economies, and highly advanced countries coming on to the same platform to discuss, and to find possible solutions for the world problems political, economic and industrial, and finally with such mutual co-operation to build global peace and world development. There is the commitment of the wealthiest and most industrialized countries of the world in one way, and along with the nations of emerging economies as well, forging ahead in their annual summits, the heads of member-states, and work for possible solutions for the world's crucial problems like economic, political, industrial, environment and many other challenges in the world. And thus, the most important 20 countries of the world build a broader international stage to build the welfare world. This led the unification of the world, the cold war also ended between the two super powers Russia and USA, which are also members of this conglomeration, and open dialogues and with the participation of many of the other countries. All member states are committed, and are working in equal terms, and with vision of development of the future world. This is the most significant turning point in the history of the whole world as instead of empires, and their expansionism, resulting in invasions and wars, it is unifying and developing mutual cooperation and developing the whole world at large.

And thus, the future world will never face war as happened in the earlier centuries and no colonial system will develop, but a peaceful world with independent nations has to exist and the process for that already started.

4. European Union is consisting of 28 member-states at the present, which is concerned for the unity and solidarity of nations of the European continent. Its prime aims are to establish political stability and economic prosperity to all

European nations with mutual co-operation and mutual coordination. It was founded by the countries namely- Belgium, France, Germany, Italy, Luxemburg and the Netherlands in 1993. Recently Britain withdrew from EU Membership and it wants to assume more freedom without much impact of EU. But in the coming future it may revive its decisions and strengthen the union.

5. African Union comprises 54 nations belonging to the African continent with prime aims-to build its integration, unity and solidarity amongst the African countries, to protect the sovereignty and territorial integrity, to promote better international understanding, and thus, to establish peace and security, and to establish democratic principles, besides addressing its various economic, social and political problems like apartheid and colonization in all countries of the continent and so on. Morocco alone is not a member of the Union.

Asia is a biggest continent. It has different regional unions.

6. Central Asian Union consisting of the membership of the countries namely Kazakhstan, Kyrgyzstan, Tajikistan, Turkmenistan, and Uzbekistan, which were the central Asian republics in the former USSR. The purpose of this also is to establish economic and political stability with mutual cooperation and collective work for the development and growth. Besides they wish to establish a free trade zone, eternal friendship between the nations and to establish peace in the region.

7. The Association of Southeast Asian Nations (ASEAN) had been established in 1967 with the membership countries namely Philippines, Malaysia, Singapore, Indonesia, Thailand for economic development and for establishing solidarity, and protecting themselves, from any foreign interferences.

8. BRICS is an organization of some counties with emerging economies, covering nearly half of world market and consisting of around half of world population, with membership of Brazil, Russia, India, China, and South Africa at the present. As these are the developing nations, and business, and rapid industrialization are to be further developed anew- they joined hands for mutual cooperation in all possible dimensions political, cultural and trade & commerce and they can easily influence the world economy without being affected by the global economic upheavals and undue dominations. Out of the 7 billion people in the world this region has 3 billion people. Some of the other countries that possibly to become the members of BRICS are Argentina, Indonesia, Turkey, Egypt, Iran, Nigeria, and Syria. They empower themselves to gain entry and say in solving international problems and to establish global peace. To establish some financial stability they have planned to establish BRICS Development Bank, which is another global financial institution at par with International Monetary Fund (IMF) and the World Bank. The main goal of it is mutual cooperation and co-ordination in all fronts namely-social, economic and political and will become a strong force in the world arena.

9. SAARC is the regional association with the countries Bangladesh, Bhutan, India, Nepal, Pakistan, Sri Lanka and Afghanistan, and its Head Quarters is located in Kathmandu, Nepal. It is the South Asian Association for Regional Cooperation with the prime ideal of political and economic cooperation in South Asia. It aims for social, economic and cultural development, with good foreign policies and diplomatic relations with United Nations Organization, European Union. Some other countries like Myanmar are interested in joining the association. Some possible future member nations are Turkey and South Africa. It has granted observer status to UNO, EU, South Korea, Iran, Russia, Mauritius, Australia, China, Japan, and United States.

It works for establishing peace and promoting prosperity by improving regional tie-ups in various fields from agriculture and industry; trade and commerce, science and technology and so on.

10. MINT: There is another small group formed earlier, consisting of Mexico, Indonesia, Nigeria and Turkey, highly populous countries with growing economy, they joined hands for mutual cooperation and coordination in all fronts at par with BRICS.

11. Union of Australasian nations: Again there was another proposal for the unification of Australia and New Zealand for harmonious development of both the nations with mutual cooperation. They were amongst British colonies before 1901 and later separated and Australia emerged. As there is close affinity and both governments work together very closely, this unification will benefit both of them. In fact both the nations are sovereign republics, but linked together in all aspects like economic, cultural, defense, immigrations, and now the unification will be more practicable and realistic for the establishing stability and achieving more prosperity.

And thus, each continent is uniting and working for sustainable development of the concerned nations of that continent or region they chose ultimately helping the whole world.

It is evident from the above study that the whole world is almost uniting for mutual cooperation and collective development, by forming continental-wise associations and then intern-continental and world associations for establishing the world peace and solidarity. The civilization of the humanity has been transformed, transforming and will be further transformed in the future. If we observe the history of civilizations of the humanity, the progress it had made from the ancient periods to the modern times of the latest that will help to predict what the future of the humanity will be. Some earliest civilizations were Indus Valley civilization in Harappa and Mohenjo-Daro Civilization in Indian subcontinent, and other civilizations that flourished in China, on the banks of Yellow River; there were civilizations that were found in Central America, South America, and in African continent. Some earliest civilization was found in Mesopotamia also. For example, the art and paintings found in Ajanta and Ellora caves, in India, Lascaux caves in France, in Spain, the stone-hinges in England and many mysterious and advanced cultures existed in the ancient world. The cave dwelling changed to land living. Compare The Egyptian Pharaohs to modern nuclear and space age life systems. The Egyptian civilization is especially marked with agriculture development, art and architecture, political administration, and militaristic strategies and cultures. With the keen insight, and with the knowledge we are gaining day by day, and the advancements that we are achieving from time to time in the human activities the world over, there are numerous turning points in the world's phenomenon. The human nature, his attitudes, his innovative capabilities, his way of thinking, his courage, his intelligence, his aspirations and ambitions in life are all in transition, with tremendous modifications in their consequence. All these are being counted for the development.

The march of time brought numerous civilizations and the march of mankind brought numerous empires emerging from several kingdoms in all the continents round the globe. There is significant progress that was made from the lore to the just past twentieth century and the present twenty-first century, which we can visualize that the process of evolution brought magnificent changes in everything in the world. The numerous turning points that occurred changed the flow of the society of the world. Consequently, new things emerged miraculously, from art to architecture; in science, engineering and technology; from ordinary war strategies to nuclear and mass destruction strategies; ordinary trade techniques to international trade practices. All this will lead the dawn of great new civilization-the golden age-the era of intelligence, and an entirely a new way of life will come in the world society.

After all what had happened, repeatedly occurred in the past was-many valorous men came and conquered various regions of the world invaded several countries and established their own empires ruled for sometime may be for some decades and their dynasties existed for some centuries, flourished well and declined, and after their fall new empires took shape and the same story repeated for millennia. Starting from Babylonian Empire, in Persia, the Achaemenid Empire or the Persian Empire, then Alexander's Macedonian Empire, its decline followed by the Roman Empire and the Greek Empire. When these two empires were at the pinnacle of glory the progress and innovation-materialistic and philosophical; artistic and architecture; culture and power; administration both civil and military were perfect and highly applauded. The half century span of golden period of Greece is remarkable in many aspects like political, cultural achievements, which were peerless in the annals of human history. In fact the great civilizations of Rome and Greece superseded all other civilizations in the world. For example, civilization of Athens and the political systems like its democratic principles were noteworthy. China had numerous dynasties namely the Han, Ming, Qin, Mongolians who established the Mongolian Empire and then Manchus also ruled the country and lastly the Qing dynasty prevailed. Then in Central America the Mayan Empire, the Byzantine Empire, the Inca Empire, the Ottoman Empire was a long standing empire established by Turks, the Islamic Empire, there existed golden period, the Umayyad Caliphate, The global empires namely The Portuguese Empire, The Spanish Empire, The French Empire were highly developed during the period of Napoleon Bonaparte, The British Empire, helped the world to grow culturally and philosophically. The Portuguese and the Spanish started the Age of Discovery. The Russian Empire, The Mogul Empire, The German Empire, and the axis powers Germany, Japan and Italy established their own empires and finally USA became the prime world power. The world over as said earlier-the world is in transition. There were several bygone kingdoms, dynasties and empires and even the global empires, which were thawed. All these dissolved in delusion. Monarchisms were well-flourished over two millennia, but that absolute monarchism became highly disfavored. That was a major turning point in the history of humanity. Instead of them miraculously by the third millennium parliamentary or constitutional monarchism evolved or otherwise democratic republics emerged. As in the twentieth century after the World War II everything changed and the independence movement spread all over the world.

Then emerged new world bodies for establishing ever-lasting peace all over the world, and transform it as a war-free world. For example:

12. The United Nations Organization: As mentioned earlier this UNO is a world body for protecting the world in all possible dimensions, which was established in 1945 after the World War II with the prime aims of establishing international peace and security, for developing friendly relations among the member nations, promoting social progress and advancement, to protect human rights and for improving the standard of living of all people on the globe. Its establishment was a great turning point in the annals of human history. And hence, there was the bill for the Universal Declaration of Human Rights that was brought in by this UNO besides many other activities for establishing world peace.

Along with this there are numerous international bodies aspiring for world peace and sustainable development the world over as mentioned earlier. For example, North Atlantic Treaty Organization (NATO) is consisting of 28 independent countries namely USA and some European countries who are interested in establishing peace in the region. NATO's essential purpose is to safeguard the freedom and security of its members through political and military means. It promotes democratic values and encourages consultation and cooperation on defense and security issues to build trust and, in the long run, and to prevent conflict. It is committed to the peaceful resolution of disputes. If diplomatic efforts fail, it has the military capacity needed to undertake crisis-management operations. The World Bank, International Monetary Fund and so on are working for the development of the world at large. And thus, the world is changing drastically with the happenings of numerous turning points towards betterment in all possible ways for further advancement.

13. The Pacific Union is a proposal for the development and integration of Pacific Islands like the Solomon Islands, Papua New Guinea, Vanuatu, Nauru, Kiribati, Tuvalu, Cook Islands, Tokelau, and Niue and countries in the Pacific Ocean namely Australia and New Zealand, to address their political, social and economic problems besides mutual cooperation and coordination with common trade practices, common currency, and establishing free trade zone in the region and thus, establishing the unity and solidarity amongst all these countries.

14. The Arab League is a regional union of independent Arabic countries with the membership of around 22 countries some of them are Egypt, Iraq, Jordan, Lebanon, Saudi Arabia, Syria and Yemen and so on. The main purpose of the union is to strengthen the relations between its member-countries, to establish safety and security, to achieve mutual cooperation and mutual help and to maintain the sovereignty of the countries concerned in all the matters of socio-economic and political aspects and culture. It took active role in resolving the regional conflicts and problems like in Palestine, Israel and Gaza conflicts and so in.

15. Caribbean Community is another regional organization with 15 members, 5 associates and 8 observers joined hands for mutual economic help and development and growth of the Caribbean nations.

16. Commonwealth of Independent States (CIS) is a regional organization after the splitting of USSR with the membership of the countries namely The Russian Federation, Belarus, and Ukraine, Armenia, Azerbaijan, Kazakhstan, Moldova, Turkmenistan, Tajikistan, Uzbekistan, Georgia for mutual cooperation and coordination.

The Pigeon of Peace,
in adoration spreads its wings around the entire world and hence
Welcomes 'The World Union'

The Emergence of the World Union (TWU)

The biological rhythm of all living beings is transforming due to the evolutionary process, resulting in newer life forms. There are numerous scientific-breakthroughs for centuries for predicting and gaining control over the natural phenomenon even. For example, the Newton's discovery led the ground work for the present space technology of twentieth century and twenty-first century as well.

And thus, eons-long process of evolution that was going on brought life forms with newer traits, and that is still continuing and will continue forever. That is in three and half billions of years span of time, the life on the earth is transforming from single cell to complex multi-cellular organisms, and further evolving astonishingly into numerous diversified biological forms, on this planet. This phenomenon continues forever even in the future. All the earliest forms of life are constrained to evolve to distinct newer un-expectable forms inevitably. As the time stands, the human body is now with perfect architecture with longest brain, and with greatest surface area of the cerebral cortex, but it has to further evolve into many other dimensions in the future. Consequently, a new species of humans will evolve with newer characters. They will be no more as they are as of now, but more intelligent, divine, and who can look at the world with a different perspective.

In fact, for centuries together all most all countries in the world were in the grip of alien rule. And frequent wars, conflicts, riots and revolutions all over the world made the humankind to struggle and strive. Monarchism predominated and prevailed in all the countries and people have to act at the wins and fancies of these monarchs, and then came the ingenious invention of 'Democracy' in Athens of the ancient Greece, where from this new concept of democracy "of the people, by the people and for the people," spread the world over. In twentieth century after a long strife, and after the two World Wars all most all countries in the world achieved independence, adapting parliamentary democracy. (See Table 2.1 below).

For about two thousand years besides rapid development in many dimensions like economic, social and political, and in scientific and technical; and technological and industrial fields as well, the whole of humanity suffered a lot transforming from dark ages, medieval to renaissance, and then of late the *'era of intelligence'* is emerging. Man himself changed from sheer ignorance to be an intellectual. In this age of intelligence the political scenario is very rapidly changing. Instead of waging war, by a country on another country, every country is aspiring mutually beneficial cooperation and collaboration of some other country for sustainable development.

That is during the last two millennia, in all countries and in all continents, there were wars at all times, but now in the place of such wars, friendship treaties are going on, consequently numerous groups of countries came into existence namely distinct continental unions, conceptual unions of political, social, economic, religious and ideological for mutual cooperation and collaboration. Among these if G24 and G77 join hands they comprise the whole world. Below is the tabulation 2.1, with many of those groups and the countries and their affiliations.

Besides, strangely, the end of the cold war, international cooperation has largely replaced competition. It has become common for countries to pool resources, from all other countries from all over the world and share the technology and scientific and industrial know-how to increase productivity around the globe.

The aspiration for the global welfare, and global cooperation, during the upcoming new age of these divine men has tremendously increased. Consequently, the world of cooperation and collaboration will dawn. The boundaries that have demarked for the countries of the world will be shifting, and even vanishing as mentioned earlier. And thus, the intervention and integration of the governments, companies, organizations, unions, associations, and the people will become common occurrence, in economic, social, political spheres all over the world. As an example, in this phenomenon, we can see the European Union, the international organization, of twenty seven individual countries, that began in 1950s, as a free trade area among six of them, which has further evolved for with the goal of involving the European political and economic integration. And thus, Europe can achieve an unprecedented level of international integration.

This will result in, the change of perception of the world, in all activities political, economic and otherwise, and that will enhance the international unity and solidarity further and further. The frontiers of the countries are constrained to change.

And thus, there will be tremendous increase of such organizations, promoting international alliances in different aspects, despite the cornucopia of countries, creeds, cultures, races, religions, spread around the globe. For example, The Association of Southeast Asian Nations (ASEAN), The Organization of Economic Cooperation and Development (OECD), North Atlantic Treaty Organization (NATO) and Warsaw Pact and so on as already mentioned.

Below is the list of 198+4+ countries, having nation-status, or territorial-status, out of which 193 countries are having independent national status, which are the member-states of UNO. The nations/territories namely, Hong Kong, Taiwan, Macau and Tibet (China); Vatican City, Kosovo and Albania (Europe) are not still members of UNO. There are many other numerous islands, territories (Not enlisted), which have no representation in the UNO. Palestine (Middle East), Abkhazia (East Asia), South Ossetia (East Asia), and the Saharawi Arab Democratic Republic (Africa) are also not members of UNO, but some of them are trying for such membership in UNO. And some nations like Vatican City etc have observer status in UNO.

Around the globe the trend is that some countries are associating for mutual cooperation and development through many unions, regional, continental wise or intercontinental wise. To mention them again for the stress and to tabulate- the African Union (AU)- It has out of 54 members, 53 countries are members and Morocco is not a member of this African Union; Asia is a biggest continent, and has different regions and has 48 countries. It has regional associations like, The Association of Southeast Asian Nations (ASEAN) with ten countries of Asia, for mutual economic growth, social progress and socio-cultural evolution; BRICS is another group, consisting of Brazil, Russia, India, China, South Africa; South Asian Association for Regional Cooperation; SAARC is an association, consisting of eight members namely, Afghanistan, Bhutan, Nepal, India, Bangladesh, Maldives, Pakistan and Sri Lanka and nine observers denoted by SAARC(O) namely Australia, Japan, USA, China, Iran, Myanmar, South Korea, and Mauritius; MINT, a small group consisting of Mexico, Indonesia, Nigeria, and Turkey with prospering economies for mutual cooperation; The North American Union (NAU) a continental group consisting Canada, Mexico and United States of America for mutual cooperation; The Union of South American Nations (UNASUR) another continental group consisting of only twelve nations Argentina, Bolivia, Brazil, Chile, Colombia, Ecuador, Guyana, Paraguay, Peru, Suriname, Uruguay, Venezuela and two with observer status namely, Mexico and Panama; The European Union (EU), is a continental group having out of 48 countries, it has only 27 countries have its membership. It is proposed that Australia and New Zealand should be united as one country with single currency and politically united. The Pacific Union (PU) with the islands in the Pacific region with sixteen member-states namely Australia, Cook Islands, FS Micronesia, Fiji, Kiribati, Nauru, New Zealand, Niue, Palau, Papua New Guinea, Marshall Islands, Samoa, Solomon Islands, Tonga, Tuvalu, Vanuatu. The Arab League (AL) has 22 Muslim nations in the Gulf and Africa and Eritrea, Brazil, Venezuela, and India have observer status in AL. The Cooperative Council of Arab states in the Gulf (CCASG) is consisting of the members are Bahrain, Kuwait, Oman, Qatar, Saudi Arabia, UAE. And thus, Asia has different regional Unions. G5 group of nations having high emerging economies namely Brazil, China, India, Mexico, and South Africa; G7 and G8 groups of countries are G7- Canada, France, Germany, Italy, Japan, UK and USA, after Russia joined and G7 became G8. G9 is a group of countries with Austria, Belgium, Bulgaria, Denmark, Finland, Hungary, Romania, Sweden, Yugoslavia for mutual cooperation; G10 group of eleven industrial nations, which are Belgium, Canada, France, Germany, Italy, Japan, The Netherlands and Sweden, Switzerland, and UK and USA to improve the borrowing capacity of IMF under General Arrangement to Barrow (GAB); G14 group of countries are emerging economies Brazil, Canada, China, Egypt, France, Germany, India, Italy, Japan, Mexico, Russia, South Africa, UK and USA. G15 is a group of developing nations and to foster mutually beneficial cooperation, it works, and it consists of the following seventeen nations namely Algeria, Egypt, Kenya, Nigeria, Senegal, Zimbabwe, India, Indonesia, Iran, Malaysia, Sri Lanka, Argentina, Brazil, Chile, Jamaica, Mexico, and Venezuela. The G20 group of nations are emerging economies and industrially advancing namely Argentina, Australia, Brazil, Canada, China, France, Germany, India, Indonesia, Italy, Japan, South Korea, Mexico, Russia, Saudi Arabia, South Africa, Turkey, UK, USA and European Union,; The G24 group of nations are in three regions. Region I is Africa- Algeria, Cote d'Ivoire, Egypt, Ethiopia, Gabon, Ghana, Nigeria, South Africa, The Democratic Republic of Congo; The Region II. South America and Caribbean, group of nations are Argentina, Brazil, Colombia, Guatemala Mexico, Peru, Trinidad and Tobago, Venezuela and the Region III. Asia- India, Iran, Lebanon, Pakistan, Philippines, Sri Lanka, and Syria, which will have common economic developmental issues to discuss with international organizations like IMF and World Bank. The G33- the group of countries are developing countries, which requires to solve and plan their problems and issues in trade and economic issues of them. To solve all those issues, they prepared befitting rule with negotiations with the World Bank. These 43 members are as given below but as quoted there should be 48 members. They are marked in the table below. The BASIC group of countries namely Brazil, South Africa, India and China are a bloc newly industrialized countries concerned world climatic changes. 3G group of countries are Global Growth Generating countries numbering to eleven. Also North Atlantic Treaty Organization (NATO) in which the countries that have affiliation are marked below. This is an alliance of 28 member states. Warsaw Pact is another treaty of friendship, and cooperation, and mutual assistance in Europe formed in 1955. There is another important group G-77 consisting of 134 member states denoted here by G-77/134, and these 134 member states are developing countries of the world to have mutual cooperation and collaboration and to have collective bargaining at UNO. This group formed at UNO itself. Organization of Economic Cooperation and Development (OECD) is an organization of thirty five countries to address their common economic and developmental problems.

Table 2.1.

This depicts the countries and their getting independence from their alien rule and associating with other countries for mutual cooperation and exchange of their expertise for sustainable development. This is a distinct feature for the whole world, as the transition is from war-mongering attitude to friendship developing stance around the world.

S.No	Continent	Country	Got Independence from	In the year	Membership/ Affiliation
	Africa-54 countries				
1.		Kingdom of	French and	1956	UNO, non- AU, AL,

		Morocco	Spain (Protectorates)		G-77/134
2.		Libya	Italy	1951	UNO, AU, AL, G-77/134
3.		Algeria	France	1962	UNO, AU, AL, G15, G24, G-77/134
4.		Mauritania	France	1960	UNO, AU, AL, G-77/134
5.		Tunisia	France	1956	UNO, AU, AL, G-77/134
6.		Mali	France	1960	UNO, AU, G-77/134
7		Niger	France	1958, 1960	UNO, AU, G-77/134
8.		Egypt	Britain	1923	UNO, AU, AL, G14, G15, G24, 3G G-77/134
9.		Chad	France	1965	UNO, AU, G-77/134
10.		Sudan	Britain	1956	UNO, AU, AL, G-77/134
11.		South Sudan	Sudan	2011	UNO, AU, G-77/134
12.		Ethiopia	Soviet Union	1995	UNO, AU, G24, G-77/134
13.		Eritrea	Italy	1993	UNO, AU, G-77/134
14.		Somalia	Britain, Italy		UNO, AU, AL, G-77/134
15.		Djibouti	France	1977	UNO, AU, AL, G-77/134
16.		Cape Verde	Portugal	1975	UNO, AU, G-77/134
17.		Central African Republic	France	1960	UNO, AU, G-77/134
18.		Congo	Marxist rule	1960	UNO, AU, G-77/134
19.		Democratic Republic of Congo, Zaire	Belgium	1960	UNO, AU, G24, G33,
20.		Rwanda	Belgium	1962	UNO, AU, G-77/134
21.		Uganda	Britain	1962	UNO, AU, G33 G-77/134
22.		Burundi	Belgium	1962	UNO, AU, G-77/134
23.		Guinea	France	1958	UNO, AU, G-77/134
24.		Gambia	Portugal, Britain	1965	UNO, AU, G-77/134
25.		Senegal, Mali	France	1960	UNO, AU, G15, G33, G-77/134
26.		Guinea-Bissau	Portuguese	1973	UNO, AU, G-77/134
27.		Kenya	Britain	1963	UNO, AU, G15, G33 G-77/134,
28.		Sierra Leone	Britain	1961	UNO, AU, G-77/134
29.		Ivory Coast	France	1960	UNO, AU, G24, G33, G-77/134
30.		Burkina Faso	France	1960	UNO, AU, G-77/134
31.		Liberia	American Colonial Society	1847	UNO, AU, G-7 G-77/134
32.		Ghana	Britain	1957	UNO, AU, G24,

					G-77/134
33.		Togo	France	1960	UNO, AU, G-77/134
34.		Benin	France	1960	UNO, AU, G33, G-77/134
35.		Equatorial Guinea	Spain	1968	UNO, AU, G-77/134
36		Nigeria	Britain	1960	UNO, AU, MINT, G15, G24, G33, 3G, G-77/134
37.		Sao Tome & Principe	Portugal	1975	UNO, AU, G-77/134
38.		Tanzania	Britain, UN	1961	UNO, AU, G33, G-77/134
39.		Cameroon	French, Britain	1960	UNO, AU, G-77/134
40.		Gabon	France	1960	UNO, AU, G24, G-77/134
41.		Seychelles	Britain	1976	UNO, AU, G-77/134
42.		Zimbabwe	Britain	1965	UNO, AU, G15, G33, G-77/134
43.		Angola	Portuguese	1975	UNO, AU, G-77/134
44.		Zambia	Britain	1964	UNO, AU, G33, G-77/134
45.		Malawi	Britain	1964	UNO, AU, G-77/134
46.		Mozambique	Portugal	1975	UNO, AU, G33, G-77/134
47.		Comoros	France	1975	UNO, AU, AL, G-77/134
48.		Madagascar	France	1960	UNO, AU, G33, G-77/134
49.		Mauritius	Dutch, French, Britain	1968	UNO, AU, SAARC(O), G33, G-77/134
50.		Namibia	South Africa	1990	UNO, AU, G-77/134
51.		Botswana	Britain	1966	UNO, AU, G-77/134
52.		South Africa	Britain, Dutch	1910	UNO, AU, BRICS, G5, G14, G20, G24, G33, G-77/134
53.		Swaziland	Britain	1968	UNO, AU, G-77/134
54.		Lesotho	Britain	1966	UNO AU, G-77/134
54 A		Sahrawi	Spain	1976	Non-UN
	Asia- 48 countries				
55.		Turkey			UNO, MINT, G20, G33, NATO, OECD
56.		Armenia	Soviet Union	1918	UNO
57.		Georgia	Russia	1991	UNO
57 A		Abkhazia	Georgia	1990, 91, 92, 99	Non-UN
58.		Azerbaijan	Soviet Union	On Collapse of USSR	UNO
59.		Israel.	Conflict with Syria, Palestine	Still continues	UNO, OECD

60.		Syria	France	1946	UNO, AL, G24, G-77/134
61.		Lebanon	France	1943	UNO, AL, G24, G-77/134
62.		Iraq	Britain	1932	UNO, AL, 3G, G-77/134

63.		Kuwait	Britain	1961	UNO, AL, CCASG, G-77/134
64.		Jordan	Peace treaty with Israel	1994	UNO, AL, G-77/134
65.		Saudi Arabia	A part of it was a Britain's protectorate	Kingdom Formed 1932	UNO, AL, CCASG, G20, G-77/134
66.		Yemen	A part of Saudi Arabia, separated End of British Rule in Yemen	1967	UNO, AL, G-77/134
67.		United Arab Emirates	Britain	1971	UNO, AL, CCASG, G-77/134
68.		Qatar	Britain	1971	UNO, AL, CCASG, G-77/134
69.		Bahrain	Britain	1971	UNO, AL, CCASG, G-77/134
70.		Kazakhstan	USSR	1991	UNO
71.		Uzbekistan	USSR	1991	UNO
72.		Turkmenistan	Russia	1991	UNO, G-77/134
73.		Oman		1997	UNO, AL, CCASG, G-77/134
74.		Tajikistan	Islamic lead opposition Supported by USSR		UNO, G-77/134
75.		Afghanistan		1919	UNO, SAARC, G-77/134
76.		Kyrgyzstan	USSR	1991	UNO
77.		Pakistan	Britain	1947	UNO, SAARC, G24, G33, G-77/134

78.		India	Britain	1947	UNO, SAARC, BRICS, G5, G14, G15, G20, G24, G33, BASIC, 3G, G-77/134
79.		Iran	Became Republic	1979	UNO, SAARC(O), G15, G24, G-77/134
80.		Maldives	Britain	1968	UNO, SAARC, G-77/134
81.		Sri Lanka	Britain	1948	UNO, SAARC, G15, G24, G33, G-77/134
82.		Bangla Desh	Pakistan	1971	UNO, SAARC, 3G, G-77/134
83.		Nepal	Republic	2008	UNO, SAARC, G-77/134
84.		Myanmar (Burma)	Britain	1948	UNO, SAARC(O); ASEAN, G-77/134
85.		Laos	France	1953	UNO, ASEAN, G33, G-77/134
86.		Bhutan	Parliamentary Monarchy	Kingdom	UNO, SAARC, G-77/134
87.		Cambodia	France	1953	UNO, ASEAN, G-77/134
88.		Vietnam	France	1954	UNO, ASEAN, 3G, G-77/134
89.		Thailand	Parliamentary Monarchy		UNO, ASEAN, G-77/134
90.		Malaysia	Britain	1957	UNO, ASEAN, G15, G-77/134
91.		Timor –Leste	Portugal -1975 Indonesia-2002	Democracy	UNO, ASEAN(O), G-77/134
92.		Brunei Darussalam	Britain	1984	UNO, ASEAN, G-77/134
93.		Indonesia			UNO, ASEAN, G15, 3G, G20, G33, G-77/134

94.		Philippines	Japan	1946	UNO, ASEAN, MINT, G24, G33, 3G, G-77/134
95.		Singapore	United Kingdom	1963	UNO, G-77/134
96.		China	No alien rule		UNO, BRICS, SAARC(O), G5, G14, G20, G33, BASIC, 3G
97.		Mongolia	China Republic	1911 1924	UNO, G33, 3G, G-77/134
98.		Hong Kong	Britain In China	1997	Non-UN
99.		Taiwan	In China		Non-UN
100.		North Korea	Still communistic country Democratic Republic Annexation by Japan in 1910 And Liberated in	1945	UNO, OECD
101		South Korea	Japan	1945	UNO, G20, SAARC(O), G77-134
102.		Japan	Constitutional Monarchy	--	UNO, SAARC(O), G7, G8, G10, G20, G14, OECD
103		Macau	Portugal	1999	Non-UN
103. A		Tibet	China	Autonomous	Non-UN
103.B		Palestine	Under British Administration till 1948	Sovereign State	Non UN, AL, G-77/134
103.C		South Ossetia	1990, 2008	Georgia	Non-UN
	Europe- 45 countries 27 countries are EU members				
104		Iceland	Denmark	1944	UNO, NATO, OECD
105		Sweden	Kingdom		UNO, EU, G10, OECD, G9
106		Norway	Kingdom		UNO, NATO, OECD
107		Finland	USSR	1917	UNO, OECD, G9

108		Denmark	Kingdom		UNO, EU, OECD, NATO, G9
109		United Kingdom and Northern Ireland	Otherwise called as Great Britain consisting of England, Scotland and Northern Ireland		UNO, G7, G8, G10, G14, G20, NATO, OECD
110		Ireland	Britain	1921	UNO, EU, OECD
111		The Netherlands	Spain Recognized	1581 1648	UNO, EU, G10, NATO, OECD
112		Luxembourg	Germany	1944-45	UNO, EU, OECD, NATO
113		Belgium	Became federal state	1994	UNO, EU,G9, G10, NATO, OECD
114		France	Republic	1792	UNO, EU, G7, G8, G10, G14, G20, NATO, OECD
115		Monaco	Principality of Monaco Constitution	1911	UNO
116		Germany	Germany united in	1990	UNO, EU, G7, G8, G10, G14, G20, NATO, Warsaw Pact, OECD
117		Switzerland	Federal State	1848	UNO, G10, OECD
118		Poland	USSR	1989	UNO, EU, OECD, NATO, Warsaw Pact
119		Czech Republic (Czechoslovakia in 1955)	Slovak Republic	1989	UNO, EU, NATO, OECD Warsaw Pact
120		Austria	Dutch, Hungary First Republic	1918	UNO, EU, G9, OECD
121		Liechtenstein	Germany	1866	UNO
122		Hungary	communistic leadership	1989	UNO, EU, G9 OECD, NATO, Warsaw Pact
123		Slovakia (In 1955 it is Czechoslovakia)	Czech Republic	1993	UNO, EU, NATO, OECD Warsaw Pact

124		Kosovo	Serbia	2008	Non-UN
125		Romania	Revolution	1989	UNO, EU, NATO, G9, Warsaw Pact
126		Bosnia &Herzegovina	Yugoslavia	1969& 1992-95	UNO, G-77/134
127		Bulgaria	Republic		UNO, EU, G9, NATO, Warsaw Pact
128		Slovenia	Yugoslavia	1991	UNO, EU, NATO, OECD
129		Croatia	Croatia-Serbs Civil war 1991-95	1995	UNO, EU, NATO
130		Serbia	Independent Republic separated from Ottoman Empire	2006	UNO
131		Alabama	Communistic rule	1991	UNO
132		Montenegro	Serbia	2006	UNO
133		Macedonia	Yugoslavia	1991	UNO
133A		Albania	Ottoman empire	1912	NATO Non-U NO Warsaw Pact
134		Portugal	Dictatorship	1948	UNO, EU, NATO, OECD
135		Andorra	France and Spain	1993	UNO
136		Spain	Present democracy	1978	UNO, EU, OECD, NATO
137		Italy	Republic	1946	UNO, EU, G7, G8, G10, G14, G20, NATO, OECD
138		Vatican City	Italy	1929	Non-UN
139		Malta	Britain	1964	UNO, EU
140		Greece	Turkey	1830	UNO, EU, NATO, OECD
141		San Marino	Roman Empire constitution	301 AD 1600 AD	UNO
142		Cyprus	Republic	1974	UNO, EU
143		Estonia	Russia	1994	UNO, EU, NATO, OECD
144		Lithuania	Russia	1990	UNO, EU,

					NATO
145		Latvia	Russia	1991	UNO, EU, OECD, NATO
146		Belarus	Soviet Union	1990	UNO
147		Ukraine	USSR	1991	UNO
148		Russia	USSR	1991	UNO, BRICS, G8, G14, G20
149		Moldova	USSR	1991	UNO
	Australia & Oceana **14 countries and numerous Islands**				
150		Commonwealth of Australia	United Kingdom	1901	UNO, SAARC(O), PU, G20, OECD
151		New Zealand	United Kingdom	1947	UNO, PU, OECD
152		Micronesia	Portugal, Spain, Cape Verde Self governing	1986	UNO, PU, G-77/134
153		Papua New Guinea	Australia	1949	UNO, PUASEAN(O), G-77/134
154		Solomon Islands	United Kingdom	1978	UNO, PU, G-77/134
155		Fiji	United Kingdom	1970	UNO, PU, G-77/134
156		Vanuatu	France, and United Kingdom	1980	UNO, PU, G-77/134
157		Kiribati	United Kingdom	1979	UNO, PU, G-77/134
158		Samoa	New Zealand	1962	UNO, PU,
159		Tuvalu	Britain	1978	UNO, PU
160		Tonga	Britain	1970	UNO, PU, G-77/134
161		Palau	USA	1994	UNO, PU
162		Marshall Islands	USA	1979	UNO, PU, G-77/134
163		Nauru	Britain, Australia and New Zealand	1968	UNO, PU, G-77/134
163 A		Niue (New	Monarch	1994	PU

		Zealand)			
	North America 23 countries				
164		Canada	United Kingdom	1867	UNO, NAU, G7, G8, G10, , G14, G20, NATO, OECD
165		United States	Britain	1776	UNO, G10, SAARC(O), NAU, G7, G8, G14, G20, NATO, OECD
166		Belize	Britain	1981	UNO, G33, G-77/134
167		Guatemala	Spanish Empire	1821	UNO, G24, G33, G-77/134
168		Mexico	Spain	1810	UNO, MINT, NAU, G5, G14, G15, G20, G24, OECD
169		Honduras	Spain	1821	UNO, G33, G-77/134
170		El Salvador	Spain	1821	UNO, G33, G-77/134
171		Cuba	USA	1902	UNO, G33, G-77/134
172		Nicaragua	Spain, Mexico, Central America	1821	UNO, G33, G-77/134
173		Panama	Columbia	1903	UNO, G33, G-77/134
174		Bahamas	United Kingdom	1973	UNO, G-77/134
175		Costa Rica	Spain	1821	UNO, G-77/134
176		Saint Kitts & Nevis	Britain	1983	UNO, G33, G-77/134
177		Dominican Republic	Spain	1821	UNO, G33
178		Jamaica	Britain	1962	UNO, G15, G33
179		Antigua & Barbuda	Britain	1981	UNO, G33, G-77/134
180		Haiti	France	1804	UNO, G33, G-77/134

181		Dominica	Britain	1978	UNO, G-77/134
182		Barbados	Britain	1966	UNO, G33, G-77/134
183		Saint Lucia	Britain	1979	UNO, G33, G-77/134
184		Trinidad &Tobago	Britain	1962	UNO, G24, G33, G-77/134
185		Saint Vincent & The Grenadines	Britain	1979	UNO, G33, G-77/134
186		Grenada	Britain	1974	UNO, G33, G-77/134
	South America				
187		Colombia	Spain	1810	UNO,UNASUR, G24, G-77/134
188		Venezuela	Spain	1811	UNO, UNASUR, G15, G24, G33, G-77/134
189		Suriname	The Netherlands	1975	UNO, UNASUR, G33, G-77/134
190		Guyana	Britain	1966	UNO,UNASUR, G33, G-77/134
191		Ecuador	Declared From Spain From Gran Colombia	1809 1822 1830	UNO, UNASUR, G-77/134
192		Peru	Spain	1821	UNO, UNASUR, G24, G33, G-77/134
193		Bolivia	Spain	1825	UNO, UNASUR, G-77/134
194		Chile	Spain	1818	UNO, UNASUR, G15, G-77/134, OECD
195		Brazil	Portugal	1822	UNO, BRICS, UNASUR, G5, G14, G20, G24, BASIC, G15, G-77/134
196		Argentina	Spain	1816	UNO, UNASUR, G15, G20, G24,

					G-77/134
197		Paraguay	Spain	1811	UNO, UNASUR, G-77/134
198		Uruguay	Brazil	1825	UNO, UNASUR, G-77/134
	Organizations/Association				
1.	European Union				SAARC(O), G20

There are numerous international inter-governmental and non-governmental organizations working for the world welfare and for sustainable development in various fields and we enlist hereunder some of them (some of which were already mentioned and discussed above). All these organizations are paving the way for the emergence of 'the World Union'. For the complete and exhaustive list of these organizations refer to *"The Year Book of International Organizations,"* published by Union of International Associations, *USA.*

There are nearly 67000 international inter-governmental organizations (IGOs) and 25000 international non-governmental organizations (INGOs) and it is difficult to enlist all of them in this book, as it is beyond its scope.

So we enlist some major existing international inter-governmental organizations (IGO) and some major non-governmental organizations (INGO) as well.

Inter-Governmental Organizations:

United Nations Organization (UNO) and its subsidiaries:

Mainly it has six important organs-

The General Assembly

The Security Council

The Economic and Social Council

The Secretariat

The International Court of Justice

The Trusteeship Council

There are four UN offices around the globe namely-

Head Quarters: United Nations Organization, New York, USA

United Nations Office, Nairobi, Kenya, Africa

United Nations Office, Vienna, Austria, Europe

United Nations Office, Geneva, Switzerland, Europe

Besides these there are some other subsidiary UN organs namely-:

International Criminal Tribunal for the former Yugoslavia (ICTY)

International Criminal Tribunal for Rwanda (ICTY)

International Residual Mechanism for Tribunals (ICMT)

The other Agencies, Programs, and Funds of UNO in different fields, which are working for the welfare of the world are-

Food and Agriculture Organization

International Labor Organization

International Civil Aviation Organization

International Maritime Organization

United Nations Convention on the Law of the Sea, international waters, and territorial waters

Joint United Nations Program on HIV/AIDS

United Nations Capital Development Fund

United Nations International Children's Emergency Fund (UNICEF)

United Nations Development Program (UNDP)

United Nations Educational, Scientific and Cultural Organization (UNESCO)

United Nations Environment Program

United Nations Human Settlements Program

United Nations Industrial Development Organization

United Nations Office for Disaster Risk Reduction (UNISDR)

United Nations Office on Drugs and Crime

Universal Postal Union

World Health Organization (WHO)

World Intellectual Property Organization

World Food Program

World Meteorological Organization

World Tourism Organization

The other international organizations in many other fields besides UNO's organizations are:

Fisheries:

Asia-Pacific Fishery Commission (APFIC)

Commission for the Conservation of Antarctic Marine Living Resources (CCAMLR)

Great Lakes Fishery Commission (GLFC)

Indian Ocean Tuna Commission (IOTC)

Inter-American Tropical Tuna Commission (IATTC)

International Commission for the Conservation of Atlantic Tunas (ICCAT)

International Pacific Halibut Commission (IPHC)

International Whaling Commission (IWC)

Network of Aquaculture Centers in Asia-Pacific (NACA)

North-East Atlantic Fisheries Commission (NEAFC)

Northwest Atlantic Fisheries Organization (NAFO)

North Atlantic Salmon Conservation Organization (NASCO)

Pacific Salmon Commission (PSC)

Southeast Asian Fisheries Development Center (SEAFDEC)

Western and Central Pacific Fisheries Commission (WCPFC

Migration:

International Organization for Migration (IOM)

International Centre for Migration Policy Development (ICMPD)

Maritime:

Antarctic Treaty Secretariat (ATS)

International Hydrographic Organization

International Maritime Organization

International Seabed Authority

International Council for the Exploration of the Sea (ICES)

North Pacific Marine Science Organization (PICES)

Environment:

Agreement on the Conservation of Albatrosses and Petrels (ACAP)

Global Environment Facility (GEF)

International Network for Bamboo and Rattan (INBAR)

Inter-governmental Panel on Climate Change (IPCC)

The International Union for Conservation of Nature (IUCN)

Partnerships in Environmental Management for the Seas of East Asia (PEMSEA)

Missing Persons:

International Commission on Missing Persons (ICMP)

Arms Control:

Organization for Security and Co-operation in Europe (OSCE)

Conference on Disarmament

Organization for the Prohibition of Chemical Weapons

Preparatory Commission for the Comprehensive Nuclear-Test-Ban Treaty Organization (CTBTO)

Wassenaar Arrangement

Nuclear Suppliers Group (NSG)

Australia Group (AG)

Missile Technology Control Regime (MTCR

Energy:

Multi Sector:

International Energy Agency

Energy Charter

Energy Community

International Institute for Applied Systems Analysis (IIASA)

International Energy Forum (IEF)

Sustainable Energy:

International Renewable Energy Agency (IRENA)

Sustainable Energy for All (SE4ALL)

Renewable Energy and Energy Efficiency Partnership (REEEP)

Nuclear Power:

European Atomic Energy Community

International Atomic Energy Agency

International Centre for Synchrotron-Light for Experimental Science Applications in the Middle East

Korean Peninsula Energy Development Organization

Nuclear Energy Agency

United Nations Atomic Energy Commission

World Association of Nuclear Operators

International Commission on Radiological Protection

Law and Justice:

Customs, Law and Enforcement:

World Customs Organization (WCO)

International Criminal Court (ICC)

International Criminal Police Organization (Interpol)

Financial, Trade and Commerce and development:

Alliance for Financial Inclusion (AFI)

African Development Bank

Asian Development Bank

Asian Infrastructure Investment Bank

Bank for International Settlements

Black Sea Trade and Development Bank (BSTDB)

Caribbean Development Bank (CDB)

Council of Europe Development Bank (CEB)

European Bank for Reconstruction and Development (EBRD)

General Agreement of Tariff and Trade (GATT)

Inter-American Development Bank

International Bureau of Weights and Measures (BIPM)

International Fund for Agricultural Development (IFAD)

International Development Law Organization (IDLO), Head Quarters: Rome (www.idlo.int)

International Monetary Fund (IMF)

Islamic Development Bank (IDB)

Netherlands Development Finance Company (FMO)

Nordic Development Fund (NDF)

Nordic Investment Bank (NIB)

New Development Bank (NDB)

OPEC Fund for International Development (OPEC Fund)

Organization for Economic Co-operation and Development (OECD)

Organization of Petroleum-Exporting Countries (OPEC)

West African Development Bank (BOAD)

World Bank Group

International Bank for Reconstruction and Development (IBRD)

International Development Association (IDA)

International Finance Corporation (IFC)

Multilateral Investment Guarantee Agency (MIGA)

International Centre for Settlement of Investment Disputes (ICSID)

World Trade Organization (WTO)

Advisory Centre on World Trade Organization Law

Industrial and Transport:

Intergovernmental Organization for International Carriage by Rail (OTIF)

International Union of Railways (UIC)

Organization for Cooperation of Railways (OSJD or OSShD)

Educational and Institutional:

Academy of European Law (ERA)

Cerlalc

Commonwealth of Learning (COL)

EUCLID (university)

European University Institute

International Bureau of Education IBE, now a part of UNESCO

International Institute for the Unification of Private Law

United Nations University

Cultural:

Commonwealth of Nations

International Centre for the Study of the Preservation and Restoration of Cultural Property ICCROM

Organization of Ibero-American States (OEI)

International Organization of Turkic Culture (TÜRKSOY)

Ethnic and Religious:

Arab League

Organization of Islamic Cooperation

Linguistic:

Organisation internationale de la Francophonie

Community of Portuguese Language Countries (CPLP)

Political:

NATO

Non-Aligned Movement

Group of 15 (G-15)

Group of 77 (G-77)

Group of 24 (G24)

Alliance of Small Island States (AOSIS)

Bolivarian Alliance for the Americas (ALBA)

New Agenda Coalition

Non-Proliferation and Disarmament Initiative[2]

Western European and Others Group

Warsaw Pact

International Institute for Democracy and Electoral Assistance (International IDEA)

Science and Technology:

The Third World Academy of Science

Japan Society for Promotion of Science

Chinese Academy of Sciences

The Polish Academy of Sciences

Royal Society, London

Commission of European Communities

Computer and Information Science

Microsoft

Assensure Ltd

And many such Multi National Companies

Continental, Regional, and Trans-Continental:

Asia:

Association of Southeast Asian Nations (ASEAN);

Asian Cooperation Dialogue

Besides these, there are numerous other organizations strengthening Asia. Some of them are-

Asian Development Bank (ADB)

East Asia Summit (EAS

Bay of Bengal Initiative for Multi-Sectoral Technical and Economic Cooperation (BIMSTEC)

Colombo Plan

Mekong–Ganga Cooperation (MGC)

Mekong River Commission (MRC)

Partnerships in Environmental Management for the Seas of East Asia (PEMSEA)

South Asian Association for Regional Cooperation (SAARC)

Southeast Asian Ministers of Education Organization (SEAMEO)

Trilateral Cooperation Secretariat (TCS)

Gulf Cooperation Council (GCC)

Africa:

African Union

Conseil de l'Entente

Economic Community of West African States (ECOWAS)

East African Community (EAC)

West African Economic and Monetary Union (UEMOA)

Southern African Development Community (SADC)

Intergovernmental Authority on Development (IGAD)

Arab Maghreb Union

Europe:

European Union (EU); Council of Europe

The other unions in this continent in all other fields:

Western European Union

Council of Europe (CoE)

Energy Community

European Free Trade Association (EFTA)

European Patent Organization (EPO)

European Science Foundation

European Organization for the Safety of Air Navigation (EUROCONTROL)

Group of 9 (G9)

International Commission on Civil Status (ICCS)

Central Commission for Navigation on the Rhine (CCNR)

Council of the Baltic Sea States (CBSS)

Baltic Black Sea Union (BBSU)

Assembly of European Regions (AER)

Eiroforum

CERN

European Fusion Development Agreement (EFDA JET)

European Molecular Biology Laboratory (EMBL)

European Space Agency (ESA)

European Organization for the Exploitation of **Met**eorological **Sat**ellites (EUMETSAT)

European Southern Observatory (ESO)

European Synchrotron Radiation Facility (ESRF)

European x-ray free electron laser (European XFEL)

Institut Laue–Langevin (ILL)

Baltic Marine Environment Protection Commission

Benelux

Belgium–Luxembourg Economic Union

British–Irish Council

Nordic Council

Nordic Investment Bank

Northern Dimension Partnership in Public Health and Social Well-being (NDPHS)

Organization for Joint Armament Co-operation(OCCAR)

Agency for International Trade Information and Cooperation (AITIC)

Visegrád Group (V4)

EUREKA

European Cooperation in Science and Technology (COST)

Community for Democracy and Rights of Nations (Commonwealth of Unrecognized States)

All these unions show how strongly the European countries are interwoven.

South America and Central America:

Union of South American Nations (USAN)

Mercosur

Andean Community of Nations

Justice Studies Center of the Americas (JSCA)

Caribbean Community (CARICOM)

Association of Caribbean States (ACS)

Organization of Eastern Caribbean States (OECS)

Central American Parliament

Bolivarian Alliance for the Americas (ALBA)

Rio Group

System of Cooperation Among the American Air Forces (SICOFAA)

Central American Bank for Economic Integration(CABEI)

Central American Integration System

Organización Latinoamericana de Energia (OLADE)

North America:

Union of North American States;

Organization of American States;

Australia and New Zealand:

Pacific Union;

Pacific Islands Forum

Transcontinental Unions

Eurasia

Asia-Europe Foundation (ASEF)

Central Asian Cooperation Organization

Collective Security Treaty Organization (CSTO)

Commonwealth of Independent States (CIS)

Economic Cooperation Organization (ECO)

Eurasian Economic Union (EEU or EAEU)

GUAM Organization for Democracy and Economic Development

Organization of the Black Sea Economic Cooperation (BSEC)

Shanghai Cooperation Organisation (SCO)

TRACECA

Turkic Council (TurkKon)

Trans-Atlantic

North Atlantic Treaty Organization (NATO)

Organization for Security and Co-operation in Europe (OSCE)

South Atlantic Peace and Cooperation Zone (ZPCAS)

Mediterranean

Union for the Mediterranean

Indian Ocean

Indian Ocean Rim Association for Regional Cooperation (ARC)

Indian Ocean Commission

Arctic Ocean

Arctic Council

Pacific Ocean

ANZUS

Asia-Pacific Economic Cooperation (APEC)

Melanesian Spearhead Group (MSG)

Pacific Islands Forum

Pacific Regional Environment Programme (SPREP)

Secretariat of the Pacific Community

African, Caribbean and Pacific Group of States

Technical Centre for Agricultural and Rural Cooperation ACP-EU (CTA)

International Non-governmental Organizations:

A few of these organizations

Amnesty International

Care International

Carnegie-Mellon Foundation

Ford Foundation

Gates Foundation

Rockefeller Foundation

Oxfarm International

Southeast Asia Treaty Organization (SEATO)

One of such prime international organization that is to be established in education for the world will be United World Educational Organization (UWEO). For complete information about it refer to [2]. Its model may be as follows:

III. United World Educational Organization[2] (UWEO)
(For global educational cooperation)

United World Educational Organization

UWEO

Unite, Unite and Unite this World and

Pledge for Peace, Progress and Prosperity of the United World

| **Home** | **Administration Membership Objectives Applications Careers** | **contact us** |

Home

The United World Education Organization (UWEO) has to be established with the foresight and planning with the sole aim of universalization of higher education for global integration, where in the UWEO institutions people learn the real life in the upcoming new world of tranquility. The value of life lies in knowing the world in its full sense, for peace, progress and prosperity and the future sustainable development of the world. So in all the UWEO institutes both adopted and accredited and of its own around the globe, these concepts of world unity will be made to be experienced by each student and member of the faculty and bring them into the fold of world unity. This UWEO will be the World's Academic Accreditation Authority, which will built up a Global University System and all its accredited institutes will strive to establish a new world order making it more congenial to live in, with full of aesthetic sense of life in all possible dimensions.

In order to develop such a tranquil world, all institutions of UWEO will strive and struggle to solve the problems of their respective countries and the whole world will turn out to be a problem free world.

While discussing with Dr. Federico Mayor Zaragoza, the then Director General of UNESCO, the idea of establishing a universal organization with the collaboration of UNESCO emerged and finally it worked out in a different way. Later the discussions went on with the UNESCO officials in 1992-93, especially Dr. M.A.R. Dias, E. Apea, V. Zharov and corresponded with Prof.Wolfgang Mitter of Germany and the experiences and visits the world over paved the way for establishing this organization.

Administration

There will be Honorary Chairmen, Chairmen on election, Deputy Chairmen, Executive Secretary, Secretary, Treasurer, and the Executive Members. There will be a Board of Trustees besides the Executive Council and the Advisory Council in the Organization.

The Board of Trustees

The Organization will run on the directions and advises given by this Board and vested the final powers of approval about all matters and every document after approval of the Board should be finally signed by the Chairman or his nominee namely the Director General (Nominated employee subordinate to the board)

There will be three Vice-Chairmen, Executive Secretary, General Secretary, Joint Secretary, and Treasurer. This 8 member group is called as the Council of the Chairman.

Besides the Council there will be 8 or 9 members to be nominated by the Chairman from this Board of Trustees.

Members of the Board will be:

1. President of USA
2. President of UK
3. President of Canada
4. President of France
5. President of Germany
6. President of Australia
7. President of China
8. President of Russian Federation
9. President of India
10. President of Japan
11. President of South Korea
12. Three Presidents of African Countries
13. Presidents of Brazil
14. President of Argentina
15. Secretary General/Director General of UNO/UNESCO

Associate Members of the Board of Trustees:: Presidents of other developing countries like Sudan, Holland, Greenland, New Zealand etc Each member will have his own representative who will act on his/her behalf in case of need. This will constitute the main Board of Trustees and the Executive Committee will be as follows:

The Executive Committee

This committee will function on the directions of the Board of Trustees and all decisions should be approved by that Board before executing them. And all the executive powers are vested on this committee

1. Director General is the supreme Executive Head of the Organization.
In charge of six sections – General Administration, Finance, Education and Curriculum, Cultures and programs, Geographical aspects, International Relations.. Each section will have one Associate DG, two Assistant DGs and computer workers as assistants.
2. Secretary General- He will be collaborating with all the people and plan the whole scheme with the association of DGs, for establishing Global Universities all over the world.
3. Associate DGs and Assistant DGs

Local Offices of UWEO
3. DDG-North America
4. DDG- Central America
5. DDG-South America
6. DDG, Russian Federation
7. DDG-Eurasia
8. DDG Europe
9. DDG-Australia-Oceana
10. DDG-East Asia
11. DDG-South-East Asia
12. DDG-South-Asia
13. DDG-South-west Asia
14. DDG-Caribbean Area
15. DDG-Africa

The Board of Trustees and The Executive council will jointly work for the welfare of this world society by using Higher Education as a powerful means of developing the new generations with universal vision and universal amity and brotherhood.

There will be another The Advisory Council, which consists of the representation from all the countries of the world willing to serve the cause of the United World Educational Organization. These members will hold the membership office by invitation and for designated time frame.

Each regional office in the organization shall have minimum of ten universities/institutes in the organization.

Fellowship/Membership

There are numerous types Honorary Fellows (On invitation), Founding Fellows (The fellows who were actively associated while establishing the Organization), Fellows, Life Members, Members. Fellowship awardees will be presented a diploma certificate with the title FUWEO and can suffix to their names. Every life member will be promoted as Fellow within one year of their life membership

The present Founding Fellows are:

1. ....25 (Enlist them)

This list is not the final but is subject to change with due modifications with the inclusions and exclusions of the founding members.

Objectives

The main objective of this United World Educational Organization is for the Universalization of Education for Global Integration

As Nelson Mandela said that the *"Education is the most powerful weapon, which you can use to change the world."*

The world needs a plan for a social and cultural transformation leading to the concepts of universalism and internationalism. This can be achieved through international institutes of higher learning. These concepts have the high potential to minimize inter-personal and inter group conflicts, which are crippling the world amity and growth.

Tirelessly we are all striving for a new world order. A world not broken up into fragments by narrow nationalistic walls, where knowledge is free and every citizen is truthful.

Still much is there to be done for the sustainable world development for which we should invent a new set up, which will assure a new social order and will help the glorious creative career of humanity as evidenced by some experiments conducted in the U.S.A., Canada and Japan and many other countries to create a new world tranquil society.

In fact education alone will help humanity stave off the dangers of war and other such destructive activity. The more rapidly educational institutions and centers of learning of global concepts grow in numbers, the sooner global unification will be well established.

If we have such education, which is purely constructive and creative, making for true intelligence and for ennoblement of character, our goal can easily be attained. Peace, prosperity and freedom cannot be created by law but by educating masses alone. So a new system of education is to be formulated for the cause of uplifting humanity, then the standard of life and existence will have sustainable development. The highly dangerous character of superstition and narrow mindedness must be changed into wisdom, and with broadened out-look of life through education of international character.

In fact, we have many institutions of higher learning in almost every country with the international aspect for the establishment of a harmonious and creative social and cultural order of global character.

But what we need is a more appropriate authority for the accreditation of the universities and institutions the world over to promote a new tranquil world enveloping the essence of universalism.

The proposed transformation can be brought about by proper education. Well planned modification of the educational set up all over the world will bring such a transformation in the three frontiers national/personal, cultural and social. And then

We transform the evils of nationalism to the élan of internationalism and establish mutual esteem and enduring friendship between nations. And thus, from the cult of nationalism emerges out the cult of internationalism or the concept of a united world.

If all people are recognized as the men of world vision with esteem of human dignity, and if there exists a closer understanding among all nations of the world then the concept of universalism will blossom like a flower in the unbounded freedom of simplicity with the limits of infinite dimensions. The whole world becomes a symbol of tolerance and universalism with the spirit of freedom and creative unity.

Many countries are coming forward for mutual co-operation and there are many such institutes for some such similar objectives but our Organization will be more practical planning and network for this objective on the global arena.

Applications

For accreditation the interested institutions can apply directly to the Head Quarters of the Organization along with all the details and their credentials, the details of foreign collaborations, financial status and courses offering, particulars of the enrollment and faculty details. After perusal of the details the concerned will be contacted for scheduling the appraisal study and on spot verification. Within three months of this study final approval and accreditation will be given after paying the due fees and award letter will be send to the institution.

Careers:

Numerous positions are in the offing and one can submit their resume to uweo1980@gamil.com. The short listed candidates will be contacted when need arises.

Contact: the Head Quarter will be at Washington D.C.

United World Educational Organization (UWEO)
Washington D.C.USA
www.uweo.org
Email: uweo1980@gmail.com

A new Universal Township, consisting of four units for the future world of peace and delight is emerging soon. This will be dealt with in the chapter viii.

IV. The Jury of the World
The International Court of Justice
(For resolving all global conflicts and confrontations)

For the law and justice, there should be some specific bodies both at the Head Quarters of 'the World Union and at the six Continental Unions Head Quarters individually. At the HQ they are 1. The World Union's Council for Law and Justice (CLJ); 2. The World Union's Court of Justice (CJ). And at the continental Head Quarters there will be similarly 1. Council for Law and Justice (CLJ), 2. The Court of Justice (CJ). They can be named as for example for the North American Continental Union (NACU), NACU Council of Law and Justice; NACU Court of Justice, similarly for the other continents. These will have jurisdiction for their continents only. And they deal with the problems of the continent within its jurisdiction, and the problems pertaining with this continent and with any other continent as well. Intercontinental problems will be dealt with by the World Union's Council of Law and Justice or World Union's Court of Justice. Similarly, at the regional level, regional set up will be there.

All agreements, treaties and understandings between any two countries about war, attack, aggression, civil disturbances, and terroristic activities will become null and void and all countries within the purview of the World Union are binding totally with the law of the Union and the continent as well.

Every country has the right to represent its issues of conflict before their continental court and if it fails there to the Union's Court of Justice.

V. The Universal Code of Conduct

The universal ideology for global acceptance and to practice both by all the nations and by all the nationals of the world

Introduction: This is an important phase for this world body namely 'The World Union' intended both for an individual, for nations welfare and for the welfare of the world, as numerous ideologies are being propounded and propagated and every individual is in a state of confusion, to which ideology is to be followed. Some ideologies are being coerced, some others are being spread with corruptive practices and some others are being spread with false promises and assurances. And some more ideologies are filled with superstitions and ignorance. The concept of universal brotherhood has lost its efficacy and effectiveness and ideas of inferiority and superiority amongst men were infused leading to an odd situation where the inferior man was asked to worship the superior man who was considered as a God incarnation resulting in conflicts and disputes. To establish harmony and happiness among men and amidst nations of the world by all possible means as it is the destiny–manifest the world over in numerous ways have been thought about.

For bringing a peaceful and tranquil world, amalgamating the best aspects from almost all existing ideologies this *"Universal Code of Conduct"* became an inevitable need of the day in the modern world. Gone were those days of war, aggression, attack for some reason or the other, and the time had ripened for peaceful living for men and peaceful coexistence for the nations the world over. And now every country and every region of it should be made livable and comfortable besides existence of natural differences.

In fact, the world is confronting with numerous problems, some are natural and many other are man-made. For the last twenty centuries, the whole world is in the grip of wars, aggressions, attacks. Terrorism is of the recent development all over the world because of ideological differences. Scholars and leaders are all searching best possible solutions for tackling this complicated situation. But even though "War against Terrorism" sprouted out it yielded no better result and those attacks are being continued somewhere or other in the world. Differences are common and natural. But adjusting to live with all differences and to live is supreme and beautiful. For that not a new ideology or not a new religion but a new way of life or a new code of conduct is desirable for this world that is to be defined and to be practiced by all people in the world and by all nations of the world.

Human diversity is inevitable and in fact needed for the world, as it is a natural phenomenon, because of environmental and geographical diversities of the world. But unity amidst the diversity is more beautiful. And everyone has to learn a new way of life to adjust with all diversities of the world.

The human life influenced much by religions propounded by various men of divine like Lord Krishna, Lord Jesus Christ, Lord Gautama Buddha, Mohammad, Mahavira, Zoroaster, Confucius, Ramakrishna Parma Hansa and Swami Vivekananda, and the list is not exhaustive. They all propounded a way of life, aiming the center as 'God', yet places they differ, they contradict, and they converge but all lead the same goal 'the God.'

All over the world there are different sects, religions, practices, and superstitions. In lieu of many of them modified forms emerged. Old philosophical concepts swayed away, and new concepts peeped in. For example, the Hindu Pantheon introduced numerous gods and numerous philosophical concepts as well. Similarly Muslims even though a single ideology "Islam" introduced by Mohammad, divided as Shiya and Sunni and now numerous concepts developed and terroristic activity has been sprouted from that precious and sacred the Islam concept. Similarly Jesus Christ introduced only one concept namely the Christianity, which has been divided into numerous denominations. Even Lord Gautama Buddha's Buddhism had suffered with division into Hinayana and Mahayana and later water downed its originality. And so is Jainism of Mahavira had the division of Digambara and Swethambara. Akbar the Great defined an amalgamated religion called Din-illahi, which couldn't gain much popularity. Of late in the nineteenth century Baha'u'llah[i, ii] founded another global religion superseding all other religions in the world called Baha'i Faith. The teachings of Ramakrishna Parama Hansa and Swami Vivekananda, Hinduism became more dynamic and popular. Amidst all these teachings of various saints the world over there is subtle similarities; apparently look different but inherently with the same sense. Hence the Baha'i[i, ii] became more popular in the present century.

Thus, this religion is one of the prime aspects for the whole of humanity influencing multi-folded forever; resulting in the peace and progress in one dimension and wars and conflicts in the second dimension, development of arts, literature, sculpture and architecture in the third dimension and thus, each religion developed its own philosophy and molded human patterns of life in another dimension. There existed and existing numerous religions and will be new religions also to be emerged and to name them some of the religions already existing are Aztec religion, Celtic religion, Greek religion, Manichaeism, Native American religion, Chinese religion, Pacific religion, Zoroastrianism, Confucianism and so on. If we consider region wise religions and a few of them are Russian religion, Mexican religion but also had Mayan religion, Japanese religion, Korean religion, Tibetan religion, Vietnamese religion, African religions, African-American religions, Australian religions, Arctic religions, Shinto religion, Taoism and so on besides famous religions like Christianity, Hinduism, Islam, Buddhism etc.

All religions aimed at the welfare of the human society and the welfare of the world and at large. If we consider the first ten popular religions and their existence in the number of countries in the world as per the above reference[1] it is as follows: The present total number of countries in the world is 238,

Religion	The number of countries it is existing
Christians	238
Non-religious	237
Atheists	219
Baha'i	218
Muslims	206
Ethno religionists	144
Jews	134
Buddhists	130
Non religionists	107
Hindus	106

United States of America has established An American Academy of Religions https://www.aarweb.org/, The AAR has thirteen staff. The office is in the Luce Center on the campus of Emory University, 825 Houston Mill Road, NE, Suite 300, Atlanta, Georgia 30329. The main telephone number is 1-404-727-3049, and the fax number is 1-404-727-7959. And its sole mission is as follows:

In a world where religion plays so central a role in social, political, and economic events, as well as in the lives of communities and individuals, there is a critical need for ongoing reflection upon and understanding of religious traditions, issues, questions, and values. The American Academy of Religion's mission is to promote such reflection through excellence in scholarship and teaching in the field of religion.

As a learned society and professional association of teachers and research scholars, the American Academy of Religion has about 9,000 members who teach in some 900 colleges, universities, seminaries, and schools in North America and abroad. The Academy is dedicated to furthering knowledge of religion and religious institutions in all their forms and manifestations. This is accomplished through Academy-wide and regional conferences and meetings, publications, programs, and membership services.

Within a context of free inquiry and critical examination, the Academy welcomes all disciplined reflection on religion—both from within and outside of communities of belief and practice—and seeks to enhance its broad public understanding.

Contemplations

There were certain contemplations in this direction by many scholars and especially by two persons namely Baha'u'llah[i, ii] and Swami Vivekananda[iv], whose reflections are important, which we will discuss.

All religions encapsulate only one universal truth, the divine truth, the man and his divine mission, the universal brotherhood, the universal love. And all religions supplement to this universal welfare and human well-being. The question of equality and inequality; meanness or greatness does not arise at all. The diversity in exposition of the same divine truth or rather the universal phenomena by distinct religions is highly an appreciable aspect but not for confrontation of each other. So we have to comprehend perfectly the crux of all ideologies, faiths and religions and practice them. Islam's excellence lies in propounding universal brotherhood, which can be followed by everyone. Christian's concept of universal love is supreme. And Hindus visualized the divinity in every living being, which is absolutely great. And thus, all these concepts are essentially needed for the mankind for building social harmony and consequently a welfare world. Hence the concept of universalism should be developed where in every ideology can be comfortably accommodated and all people live in serene environment. From that concept of universalism emerge a code to be followed by one and all and by all nations of the world.

Baha'u'llah[i, ii]: The religion once did a lot of good and bad and now it's very concept is constrained to change. With various ideologies developed, the 'unity in diversity' also developed in this modern day world.

As each religion do have its own concept for example Confucianism focused on how human beings should behave in the society and strived to identify the ideal way of life; the Egyptian religion gave importance to afterlife besides the present way of life; the Greek religion concentrated the social life that was tuned to the political way of life but the latest religion Baha'i[i, ii], which has been propounded by Baha'u'llah[i, ii], is striving to unite all people in the world spiritually.

The Baha'i[i,ii] Faith is the youngest, the fastest growing and the latest of all faiths among the religions and faiths and independent of all other religions of the world, with the sole principle of establishing peaceful, sustainable and justifiable world with the sole motto of "The oneness of God, the oneness of human family and the oneness of religion." Its membership is widely open beyond any restrictions and at one's own free will. Everyone is welcome to join a path of service and spiritual communion. It is the second most wide-spread, superseding every religion except Christianity. Its admiration is because of its nature of spearheading towards the ideal of world citizenship. It is miraculously well diverged and distinct but very well united and organized group of people on the earth.

Its founder Baha'u'llah[i, ii] (1817-1892), a Persian noble princely person from Tehran who said, "The earth is but one country and mankind its citizens and that, as foretold in all the sacred scriptures of the past, now is the time for humanity to live in unity." It is a soul stirring message of peace and unity for building up harmonious human society. He stood amongst the divine men or divine messengers on the globe like Lord Jesus Christ, Lord Krishna, Lord Gautama Buddha, Confucius, Zoroaster, Mohammad, and Abraham and he as a recent addition to the list.

In this day, as Bah'u'llah[i, ii] said that - The humanity has collectively come of age. As foretold in all of the world's scriptures, the time has arrived for the uniting of all peoples into a peaceful and integrated global society. "The earth is but one country and mankind its citizens," He wrote.

The youngest of the world's independent religions, this Faith founded by Baha'u'llah[i, ii] stands out from other religions in a number of ways. It has a unique system of global administration, with freely elected governing councils in nearly 10,000 localities.

It takes a distinctive approach to contemporary social problems. The Faith's scriptures and the multifarious activities of its membership address virtually every important trend in the world today, from new thinking about cultural diversity and environmental conservation to the decentralization of decision making; from a renewed commitment to family life and moral values to the call for social and economic justice in a world that is rapidly becoming a global neighborhood.

Thus, the central theme of Baha'u'llah's[i, ii] message is that- "the whole humanity is one single race and the day has come for the unification of the humanity into one global society." So Baha'i s believe in the following principles namely:

➢ The oneness of humanity
➢ The common origin and unity of purpose of all religions in the world
➢ The harmony of science and religion
➢ Equality of men and women
➢ The elimination of all forms of prejudices in the world
➢ The spiritual solutions to all economic problems in the world.
➢ The establishment of a world commonwealth of all nations of the world.

It was originated hundred and fifty years ago by hard efforts of Baha'u'llah[i, ii], which spread all over the world by now and its members are from distinct nations, distinct ethnic groups and distinct economic and cultural back grounds representing the whole world's humanity forming as a single community without factions, groups or splits of any kind. Its unifying vision about the nature and the world society besides the goal of life of every human being on earth are highly regarded by the present world community. The vital concern for Baha'i is the world peace. As Baha'u'llah[i, ii] says that- "world peace is not only possible but is inevitable".

Now to quote Baha'u'llah[i, ii] as- "If the learned and worldly-wise men of this age were to allow mankind to inhale the fragrance of fellowship and love, every understanding heart would apprehend the meaning of true liberty, and discover the secret of undisturbed peace and absolute composure."

As the natural process of evolution in the human thinking patterns, they vexed with so many calamities and catastrophes in the world with wars both economic, religious, ideological, ethnic, civil, social and political and it is really now in this twenty first century it is the dawn of the time for peace and tranquility the world over for such a change. So this new concept acceptable by one and all came into its existence aiming for the welfare of the humanity to live in harmony.

The highest significance of this Faith is "unity" without promoting any group or sectarian feelings amidst the community as many others like social, political or religious aspects did.

In the annals of history of mankind the concept of 'God' had the highest and tremendous impact on human mind and on name of God many faiths, ideologies and religions came into the fabric of human society, followed by numerous superstitions and dogmas peeped in unbelievably. In the other way, some of these religions were much concerned about the welfare of the human society, the peoples' life patterns and their development and growth in all possible directions.

And this faith is really well advanced concept as it strived, struggled and stressed amidst turbulent situations for the global unification, beyond caste, creed, race, religion, or region, which led for the universal civilization and creation of new world.

For establishing such global society and to get it flourished well, Baha'u'llah[i, ii] said that it must be based on certain fundamental principles. They include the elimination of all forms of prejudices; full equality between the sexes; recognition of the essential oneness of the world's great religions; the elimination of extremes of poverty and wealth; universal education; the harmony of science and religion; a sustainable balance between nature and technology; and the establishment of a world federal system, based on collective security and the oneness of humanity.

Baha'is around the world express their commitment to these principles chiefly through individual and community transformation, including the large number of small-scale, grassroots-based social and economic development projects that Bahá'í communities have launched in recent years.

In building a unified network of local, national, and international governing councils, Baha'u'llah's followers have created a far-flung and diverse worldwide community — marked by a distinctive pattern of life and activity — which offers an encouraging model of cooperation, harmony and social action. In a world so divided in its loyalties, this is in itself a singular achievement. Full information about this Baha'i Faith can obtained from the websites i, ii.

Swami Vivekananda[iv] (1863–1902) felt the need of a universal religion for the sake of the world unity, and advised to accept all religions equally. He says that all religions have the same ultimate goal of realizing God, may be having different approaches. Man is divine and the realization of that divinity is the final mission of man, the very purpose of life. That is the crux of every religion. One can realize the divinity by controlling of the mind, work selflessly, developing knowledge and wisdom, and loving the world means loving the god. Not just to tolerate but accept every ideology, every theory, to go in depth of that and if one practices it and that entire thing makes you to reach the ultimate goal without fail. In that achieving the highest aspiration where is the time for any other activity. Man will be broadened in his outlook, the whole world will be his, he will embrace the entire globe whole heartedly, but not any part of it as a region or a nation, and he can no more be, with partisan attitude.

And the breaking the narrow barriers of religion, a new code of conduct will have to emerge for the whole of the world. That will be the inevitable future developmental phenomenon.

In fact, acceptance of numerous religions is otherwise called religious pluralism, inter-religion concept, inter-faith or religious tolerance, all of which will promote the world peace and the world harmony. It will minimize the ideological differences the world over. And miraculously in this well changed world, the life styles also rapidly change, consequently life priorities too will be changed in the man's schedules. People belonging to various religious groups living and working together, forgetting their own differences, as it became inevitable. So the roots of their culture, economic status, and the social strata, will be changed. In addition to this the concept of higher education will change its attire. It will cross the borders of the nations and spread world-wide and the students are being exposed to various environments, with all adjustments with various people and thus, became more broad-minded, neglecting all types of differences and disparities whatever may it be. The once propounded inter-religious order comes into its being in the practical life of all. What Swami Vivekananda[iv] contemplated once, will emerge into the world society. All religions are acceptable by all with some exceptions by some people. Rapid social evolution constraining the further modifications in the life and living styles of man of the day. Gone are those of days of religious wars, and persecutions. The need has arisen to follow a way of life to be defined anew by the world intellectuals and scholars of the world. That is this *universal code of conduct.*

Swami Vivekananda[iv] said on September 1st, 1893 that , "But if there is ever to be a universal religion, it must be one which will hold no location in place or time; which will be infinite, like the God it will preach; whose Sun shines upon the followers of Krishna or Christ, saints or sinners, alike; which will not be the Brahman or Buddhist, Christian or Mohammedan, but the sum total of all these, and still have infinite space for development; which in its Catholicity will embrace in its infinite arms and find a place for every human being [...] It will be a religion, which will have no place for persecution or intolerance in its polity, which will recognize a divinity in every man or woman, and whose whole scope, whose whole force, will be centered in aiding humanity to realize its divine nature." He explained the ideal of such universal religion, which was the unity in all aspects of human life. The distinct faiths of the world will have to converge into one faith, which is impossible in one way. Bringing out one universal philosophy from the complex ideologies as the day stands is far from possibility as they are powerful fundamentalists opposing the progressive thinking and obstructing such moves. But one way out is by accepting all concepts and bring "Unity in Diversity", that is accepting the variation but find in it the subtle concepts of unifying aspects. A fact may be expressed in distinct ways but in reality it is only one truth and so the divine fact of the existence of God can also be expressed. Men tried to amalgamate all such distinct concepts and bring out one universal concept but in vain everywhere. In the language of love, if all men are brought together with pure and pious feelings of love, love thyself, love thy neighbor, love the world, and love the God, it is only one truth and it will bind all men, it will bind all nations and it will bind the whole world. Whoever may the God, love Him. He is at the center of the circle of all concepts are on its infinite radii. Love Him from the core of your heart from which ever radius you like silently with closed eyes and see the whole world with your open eyes with the same love. Wonderfully you visualize a different united world. We can observe that when the evil men and the evil acts decrease in the state, then the state will flourish well and so the world as well. That is when injustices creep in between men and their leaders, between countries by the fault of the respective leaders, and then the stability of peace disappears. Hence politics should move on the path, which is right and rational, keeping an eye on the welfare state. The selfish motives of the men are subsided and service oriented thinking is developing, and the world is on the path of transition for peace, progress and prosperity. For the establishment of harmonious and peaceful world, men's thinking pattern will widen and there will be progressive civilization all over the world. Thus, this universal law of the world union promotes peaceful coexistence of all countries of the world. Instead of making use of politics to your advantage, make use of it to the advantage of the people in the state that builds a better state and consequently, a better world. This stems from the fact that there is political wisdom amongst men of today and consequently, amidst the nations in the world. The political edifice so far existed will be constrained to transform into a new system, more congenial and comfortable to all men and all nations of the world.

In the world there are men with entirely different concepts of life, with different psychologies. It is impossible to make them all to think alike. For example a poet, a philosopher, a scientist, missionary men and so on are all thinking distinctly. To bring unity among them all is not that much easy as their way of life and living are different. Hence we need such unifying factor. That is-

Universal code of conduct:

Universal Code of Conduct for the individuals

> Develop universal solidarity and brotherhood and thus, the unity of the whole humanity
> Respect religion, every religion, it is a way of life to follow with unity of all religions
> Hate none but love everyone, love the society, love your country and love the world
> Do not suppress, oppress or belittle others; honoring others means honoring yourself
> Be well concerned and benevolent towards the suffering, the aged, the women and children with poise
> Be contented, with self control; never be angry and be truthful and trustworthy
> Help yourself, and help others to the best of your ability without anticipating any returns,
> Develop mutual cooperation, coordination and collaboration
> No ideology can be coerced, religion and science should be well-synthesized for the life and its development
> Freedom, liberty and justice should be prime factors of everyone's life, relinquish all prejudices
> Do not preach precepts without you practicing and serve the humanity by all means
> Be loyal to your family, to the country and to the world, and be responsible to this world of yours
> Be righteous and noble, and be pure and pious and have ethical values with honesty
> Everyone should preserve the nature as best as he can, should not mis-utilize the natural resources

- Fight not with anyone, but behave amicably, and develop right and rational thinking
- Develop inner peace and joy by having wisdom and right knowledge, and be virtuous
- Every individual should work for the welfare of the society
- Cooperate in finding solutions for all social, economic and political problems of your country and the world as well.
- No person should infringe the rights of others, what so ever, in any way.

Universal code of conduct for the countries

- No country should even try to wage a war, attack or aggression on any other country
- No country should meddle in the domestic affairs of any other country, uninvited. No nation should interfere with either external or internal problems of any other nation without invitation.
- Every country should strive for peaceful coexistence, with amity and friendship with all other countries
- Every country should live with other countries with mutual cooperation, mutual coordination
- Any country can collaborate in research and development with any other country at free will
- Any country can collaborate with any other country with absolute freedom in scientific, technological, industrial and agricultural developmental activities.
- No country should cross the borders of any other country illegally
- No country should obstruct or exploit the natural resources of any other country
- Every country can maintain its own sovereignty and allow other countries to maintain their own sovereignty
- Every country should follow strictly democratic principles, and take peoples' referendum whenever needed.
- No country can use any weaponry, military power on any other country at any time
- Every country should minimize its defense budget by all means, and support the Union absolutely
- No country should acquire nuclear, chemical and biological weaponry, and pile up
- Every country should enter into Nuclear Proliferation Treaty with the Union and strictly adhere to it
- Each nation is responsible for the world and the world is responsible for every nation of the world.
- Every country should bind over with this code of conduct inevitably, and follow it strictly.
- Every country should obey the charter of the World Union
- Every country should be promptly pay the Unions contributions without fail
- All countries should cooperate for the establishment of united world, through this Union
- No country should take reins of power of any other country in any means, what so ever may they be except in grave situations with the direction of TWU, then it should be restored as early as possible
- No country should hoard arms, maintain military, and organize any military training camps as the Union is in-charge of safety and security. All military alliances between any two countries are prohibited.
- No nation should maintain suicide squads, human bombs and such training camps either in their own or in any other country.
- The act of spying by all means by nations is strictly prohibited by the Union
- This Union is built up strictly on the principles of democracy, and all member-states should follow the same democratic principles.
- This constitution is strictly republican with powerful judiciary, and on its direction its legislation will work.
- Every country should concentrate on its own development by all means at all times, and cooperate with others also.
- Every nation should strive to built a welfare world society
- For any new concept or interpretation of any existing concept of religion, faith, ideology is to be brought in, or is to be included in this list, the prior approval and acceptance of the World Union is to be taken by the concerned that is mandatory.

This code will help-to fulfill the prime slogan of the "World Union", as

Unite, all nations of the world
Unite, the whole humanity of the world.

Plato says that, 'the just men with good morality and prudent conduct will transform their state, as just state,' and all these just states make a just continent and these just continents will make a just world. Plato pronounced that such just citizens, absolutely needed for building up a welfare state, by dealing with the political set up of the state, even in those ancient times, and all those concepts hold good in the present day world society, to get it transformed to the welfare world society. As due to the evolutionary mechanism, things changed in almost all fields and in the political system as well, and these evolutionary changes are remarkable when compared to the things of the ancient times. There was a significant advancement, and such advancement is going on rapidly and will be even in the future such advancement will occur inevitably. The growth of the world depends on the countries growth and the countries growth depends on the growth of the citizens, who will ultimately built a well ordered state, that will built a well ordered world society. For this, all states should be virtuous, with all pervading justice, and the time has been ripened for such a transformation in the world, as all men being virtuous, prudent, with temperance, and courage, such that the society will be perfect, contributing for building up a better state and consequently, a better world. In fact, if the every state is wise and the world will also be wise. In such a wise and just society, of the state or the world, every citizen has to work for the state and for the world directly and indirectly, but positively. With the well ripened wisdom, all the citizens, the state and consequently the whole world will move on the perfect path of progress and prosperity. This interlinks between the citizens and the world will be entirely fulfilled if the universal code of conduct is followed by both the individuals and the nations all over the globe.

Everyone in the world has his own freedom and liberty to live as he likes without affecting other's independence and none can coerce others to change their thinking pattern or ideological concepts. It would be social evolutionary modification in the world to have a universal code of conduct for both the nations and the nationals as well in the world and thus, it will be for the good of mankind. It is highly practicable solution for all ideological and religious conflicts in the world of today. All of we have to inculcate universal love and universal brotherhood. Then man becomes perfect. And that will result in seeing divinity in every living being. That will be the ideal reality and final goal of man. That is the eternal knowledge man has to attain, the eternal existence he has to achieve. Inherently, all distinctions and disparities disappear in the world and the universal equality will be ushered in, a modern world of peace and tranquility will emerge.

Conclusion: In fact for centuries this concept of *universal code of conduct* has been thought about. Now the time has ripened, living concept of man sophisticatedly changed, with all acceptances and adjustments within distinct ideological disparities. This universal ideology can be adapted by anyone and everyone, without affecting their own, which is totally based on the unity of the whole of mankind. This will promote more strongly the motto mentioned in the preamble of 'the World Union,' which states that

*"Universal Solidarity and brotherhood with Mutual Cooperation and Co-ordination,
Amongst all people in the world, and amidst all nations of the world."*

This principle of the code of conduct for universal solidarity and brotherhood and universal love, when followed by one and all, the world will advance economically, socially and politically without fail. And then the world unity will be ushered in.

VI. Some Existing Intercontinental Organizations and their associated countries

(For concerned regional countries' economic cooperation)

A group of countries in a continent or different continents may form a separate organization with the approval of both the World Union and Continental Union for their own conveniences and benefits without hampering the interests of the main bodies namely the World Union or the concerned Continental Union.

Now numerous international organizations developed and are developing for this purpose of mutual cooperation and mutual coordination. As already discussed earlier, the North Atlantic Treaty Organization (NATO), G_{20}, G_5, BRICS, SAARC, and numerous other united world organizations, and so on are all striving to build up the world unity and solidarity with mutual cooperation and mutual coordination.

Table 6.1

This reveals some of the present organizations and the countries affiliated to them

		The Present unions and groups And their participating countries				
G-5		Inter-continental Unions				
G-5: A group of advanced and industrialized countries namely USA, UK, France, Germany and Japan ============ The list members of G-77 is 134 for common good of the world is as follows:	G-6, G-11	G-7, 3G, G-15	G-8, G-13	G-20, G-24	NATO	Warsaw P
	G-6: A group of six advanced economies namely France, West Germany, Italy, Japan, United Kingdom and United States., G-5+ Italy ============ The Group G-11 countries, which are 11 developing but lower income groups formed as G-11 consisting of the following countries namely- Jordan, Croatia, Ecuador, Georgia, El Salvador, Honduras, Indonesia, Morocco, Pakistan,	G-7: A group of seven advanced economies namely Canada, France, Germany, Italy, Japan, United States and United Kingdom G-5+ Canada and Italy ============ 3G: with the non G-20 member nations, 28 countries planned to group again with many smaller and third world nations as Global Governance Group named as 3G group	G-8: A group of highly industrialized countries namely- France, Germany, Italy, The United Kingdom, The United States, Canada and Russia to foster consensus on global issues	G-20: A group of 19 individual nations and European Union namely Argentina, Australia, Brazil, Canada, China, France, Germany, India, Indonesia, Italy, Japan, Republic of Korea, Mexico, Russian	North Atlantic Treaty Organization (NATO) A group of 28 independent nations namely: Albania, Bulgaria Belgium, Canada, Croatia, Czech	Warsaw P Countrie associate Bulgaria East Germany Hungary Poland, Romania Soviet Uni

	Paraguay and Sri Lanka. The G-77 group of countries consists of 133 members of United Nations joined hands for mutual development: Namely- Afghanistan, Algeria, Angola, Antigua and Barbuda, Argentina, Bahamas, Bahrain, Bangladesh, Barbados, Benin, Bhutan, Bolivia, Bosnia and Herzegovina, Botswana, Brazil, Brunei Darussalam, Burundi, Cambodia, Carbo Verde, Chile, China, Colombia, Comoros, Congo, Costarica, Coted'Lvoire, Cuba, Democratic Republic of Congo, Djibouti, Dominica, Dominican Republic, Ecuador, Egypt, El Salvador, Equatorial Guinea, Eritrea, Ethiopia, Fiji, Gabon, Gambia, Ghana, Grenada, Guatemala, Guinea, Guyana, Haiti, Honduras, India, Indonesia, Iran, Jamaica, Jordan, Kenya, Kuwait, Peoples Democratic Republic of Lao, Lebanon, Lesotho, Liberia, Libya, Madagascar, Malawi, Malaysia, Maldives, Mali, Marshall Islands, Mauritania, Mauritius, Micronesia, Mongolia, Morocco, Mozambique, Myanmar, Nauru, Nepal, Nicaragua, Niger, Nigeria, Omen, Panama, Paraguay, Peru, Philippines, Qatar, Rwanda, Saint Kitts and Nevis, Saint Lucia, Saint Vincent and the Grenadines, Samoa, Saudi Arabia, Senegal, Seychelles, Sierra Leone, Singapore, Solomon Islands, Somalia, South Africa, Sri Lanka, State of Palestine, Sudan, Surinam, Swaziland, Syrian Arab Republic, Tajikistan, Thailand, Togo, Trinidad and Tobago, Turkmenistan, Uganda, United Arab Emeritus, United Republic of Tangenia, Uruguay, Vanuatu, Bolivarian Republic of Venezuela, Vietnam, Yemen, Zambia, Zimbabwe.	================== G-15 is a group of 15 countries but had been extended to 17 developing countries for international cooperation and collaboration namely Algeria, Egypt, Kenya, Nigeria, Senegal, Zimbabwe, India, Indonesia, Iran, Malaysia, Sri Lanka, Argentina, Brazil, Chile, Jamaica, Mexico, and Venezuela	like: Economic growth, global security, energy and terrorism ===== G-8+5- G13 group of nations namely- Brazil, Canada, China, France, Germany, India, Italy, Japan, Mexico, South Africa, the United Kingdom, and the United States and European Union A stronger group for international cooperation (Russia joined but was suspended)	Federation, Saudi Arabia South Africa, Turley, United Kingdom, United States and the European Union (EU) ===== G-24 group A group of 24 countries had been established for the for international co-ordination and cooperation namely- Algeria, Argentina, Brazil, Colombia, Democratic Republic of Congo, Egypt, Ethiopia, Gabon, Ghana, Guatemala, India, Iran, Ivory Coast, Lebanon, Mexico, Nigeria, Pakistan, Peru, Philippines, South Africa, Sri Lanka, Syria, Trinidad and Tobago, Venezuela. China was a special invitee.	Republic, Denmark, Estonia, France, Germany, Greece, Iceland, Hungary, Italy, Latvia, Lithuania, Luxembourg The Netherlands, Norway, Portugal, Poland, Romania, Slovakia, Slovenia, Spain Turkey, USA, UK
			BRICS- the	

				countries are Brazil, Russia, India, China, and South Africa		

VII.The World Union's Continental and Sub-Continental and Regional Unions
(For the concerned areas' growth and development, progress and prosperity)

The time has ripened for the united world erasing the border lines of all nations and subduing all differences amidst nations. And if at all there are any, they should be pacified and subsequently nullified by sheer peaceful negotiations only. In the earlier centuries in the world and amongst different countries there were invasions that were so frequent and common as a king wants to become an emperor, and an emperor wants to expand his empire further. And the way for fulfilling their ambition was invasion of other countries only. One has to conquer another country for achieving his ambition of becoming as an emperor. And thus, the world moved afar. But the major change of political concept is ending the system of monarchism and it is being replaced by 'Democracy', which is an ingenious concept that took shape perfectly by now and being followed in the world by the majority of the countries of the world. Even if there are some monarchs in some of the countries, but they are constitutional monarchs or parliamentary monarchs.

And thus, another important point in the present modern world is of developing congenial relationship with mutual cooperation and understanding. No country wants any power on any other country and no country wishes to establish their colonies in another country as occurred in the earlier times.

Table 7.1.

The new continental unions will be formed modifying the existing unions as follows:

North American Continental Union (North American Union)	South American Continental Union (Union of South American Nations, UNASUR)	African Continental Union (African Union)	European Continental Union (European Union)	Asian Continental Union	Australian & New Zealand Continental Union (Union of Australian Nations)
North American-sub-continental Union	South American Sub-continental Unions	African Sub-continental Unions	European Sub-continental Unions	Asian Sub-continental Unions	The Pacific Union
Caribbean Community			Commonwealth of Independent States (CIS)	SAARC	
				MINT	
				Central Asian Union	
				The Association of Southeast Asian Nations (ASEAN)	
				The Arab League	

These existing organizations and unions are resolving for the formation of those new unions, constituting of all the countries in the continent for their establishment and in support of 'the World Union' as mentioned above, with the sole aim of Universal solidarity and brother hood with mutual cooperation and mutual coordination. They further resolve for the formation of concerned regional unions as well. The other associations or unions will either merge with the concerned regional or continental unions or continue its being and can work for their aims and goals separately. But they are welcome to maintain cordial relations with 'the World Union' and its constituent unions as well. All these new unions will work with unity, the sustainable development of each and every nation of the world and the very world itself. The combined efforts will benefit all people in the world in many dimensions.

VIII.The World Union

(For Universal solidarity and brotherhood, and for the development of the world entire)

The concept of world is the one existed even in the Indian scriptures as it was mentioned in Hitopadesa in Panchatantra as the sloka says-

"अयं बन्धुरयं नेति गणना लघुचेतसाम् | उदारचरितानां तु वसुधैव कुटुम्बकम् || "

ayaṁ bandhurayaṁ nēti gaṇanā laghucētasām | udāracaritānām tu vasudhaiva kuṭumbakam ||

The meaning of that says that- he is my man that man is a stranger, but the magnanimous and the noble say that he himself belongs to the whole world as a family. It reveals that not only about the peace and harmony of the whole world, but everyone belongs to the whole world and all men in the world have to live as one family. How greatly it had been said implicitly the universal solidarity and brotherhood?

The electronic technology of the day's advancements made the globe to shrink in terms of transportation and communication as a village, from which sprouted the concept of the 'Global Village.' The world society has gone further with the newer concept of 'Global Theater.'

After advent of computer technological applications in almost all fields this concept furthered into 'Globalization' in almost all fields changing the world scenario greatly. This 'Globalization' in fact is a recent development influenced almost all fields remarkably, for example, academics- research, universities and colleges and all educational institutions at all levels, libraries and dissemination of knowledge; Administration and immigration; media and journalism, printing and publishing, and industry, and so on.

This 'Globalization' also influenced trade, business and commerce; banks and financial institutions; financial transactions, capital investments; Socio and cultural activity; movie field; climate and weather management activity also associated with this globalization. And the recent origin is the internet, World Wide Web, Mobile Phones with numerous Applications, which revamped the world over.

The practice of globalization existed even in fourteenth and fifteenth centuries and the long Silk Road connecting Asia, Africa and Europe testifies this. Slowly the globalization became a synonym for one world society. The process of this globalization has grown tremendously in the fields of education, law, tourism and so on.

It was in fifteenth century AD, the concept of international law had been introduced by Francisco de Vitoria[6], who further conceived the concept of "The Republic of the Whole World," knowing about the incessant wars among different nations, and in order to study deep the cause of these, he developed a theory to understand the basis of these wars, which may be in human authority. Vitoria considered power as such, just and legitimate and follows that no human will or universal agreement can dissolve it: any sort of human or chaotic anarchy that would seek to eliminate all power would constitute an affront to nature. Lastly, the immediate and mediating source of this divine power is the people from them comes the society, the community and the civil authority. Vitoria vehemently declares that instead of transfer of this power from the people to the rulers the democracy is preferable in which people will participate in the country's political affairs actively. That bestows individual freedom. He developed this concept with broader vision comprising all nations of the world that laid the foundation for the Society of Nations, which can supersede the present United Nations Organization. He furthered this idea as-its basis lies in the inescapable and inalienable unity among all peoples and races, one grounded in the human nature that is conferred without distinction on all persons. The humanity itself, from its grouping into different nations, must seek its common good, and work to preserve, to defend, and to organize itself in ways that it considers most appropriate. Nevertheless, the time might come when government by isolated and divided nations may no longer suffice to ensure the security of human nature; indeed, the time might come when some form of universal government would be perceived as the most advantages and appropriate solution. Vitoria further observed that the human race had the right to choose a single ruler in the beginning before the division of peoples and nations. It can still do so now, as this power, as a natural right, does not disappear. This solution is always available because the political authority is rooted in human nature, and the political authority can be prescribed in various, legitimate forms that express the will of citizens."As of the moment that republic possesses the right to administer itself that which is done by the majority, is that which is done by all." And thus, by considering the unity of all people, consequently, the international political unity, Francisco de Vitoria[6], conceived the concept of "The Republic of the whole world." even though it was difficult to achieve it then, but now after passage of nearly four and a half to five centuries, the time has ripened for establishing such an international political authority by name "the World Union."

It was in nineteenth century Joseph Smith[ix] and others propounded 'Theo democracy' and his council to rule as a World Government leading to the Kingdom of God, that law developed further the concept of democracy by the then intellectuals simultaneously. And in 1811 AD a German philosopher Karl Krause (1781-1832 AD), in his article entitled, "Archetype of Humanity" suggested the five continents namely Europe, Asia, Africa, America and Australia were to be the five states of World Republic, which unifies the whole world one-way.

The sublime change in the world will be the emergence of the **World Union,** with six continental unions namely North American Continental Union, South American Continental Union, African Continental Union, European Continental Union, Asian Continental Union, and Australia & New Zealand Continental Union in lieu of the existing unions like European Union, African Union, North American Union, South American Union, Unions of Asia, Union of Australia and New Zeeland.

The Arctic and Antarctic regions belong to the world, called the world regions. Each continental union will have continental sub-unions, Regional Unions and the some specific unions will also associate with the concerned continental unions.

The World Union will have one commanding currency system. The World Union's Development Bank, The World Union's Court of Justice, The World Union's University, and Universal Passport for the world citizens, the competent and deserving people will be bestowed with this honor of the world citizenship, which is highly respectable and prestigious, by the World Union and to be accepted by all continents, and hence, all countries of the world. The World Union will have their own the World Union Military System with all the latest weaponry to command any erring nation with the support of all continental unions, and hence, all nations in the world. Each continental union will have one currency, free trade zone, and free passport zone, one Continental Court of Justice, One Continental University, One Continental Development Bank, and the Continental Military System. The world will dissolve into just six continents as six united units only, which will be having the binding forces of some inter-continental unions and all are associated with the World Union. If any dispute arises between distinct nations of a continent, the concerned continental union will resolve them by peaceful negotiations and treaties. If not resolved by that continental union, it will be referred to the World Union. Its verdict will be final, if not it will direct the nation and the concerned continent what is to be done. As a last resort it alone empowered to take any military action or any other drastic action. As mentioned earlier the existing continental unions and sub-continental unions with their constituent nations are as follows:

Table 8.1

		The existing Continental Unions and their associated countries				
North American Union This being formed with Canada, Mexico and United States of America	Union of South American Nations, UNASUR- a group of 12 nations namely Bolivia, Colombia, Ecuador, Peru, Argentina, Brazil, Paraguay, Uruguay, Venezuela, Chile, Guyana, Surinam	Central American Integration System SICA Belize, El Salvador, Guatemala, Honduras, Nicaragua, and Panama. Mesoamerica And Dominican Republic	African Union 54 African nations except Morocco	European Union, EU Austria Belgium Bulgaria Croatia Cyprus Czech Republic Denmark Estonia Finland France Germany Greece Hungary Ireland Italy Latvia Lithuania Luxembourg Malta Netherlands Poland Portugal Romania Slovakia Slovenia Spain Sweden United Kingdom	Asian Unions	Union of Australian Nations
		Sub-Continental Unions				
Caribbean Community	South American Sub-continental Unions		African Sub-continental	European Sub-continental	Asian Sub-continental	The Pacific Union

				Unions	Unions	Unions	
					Commonwealth of Independent States (CIS)	SAARC	
						MINT	
						Central Asian Union	
						The Association of Southeast Asian Nations (ASEAN)	
						The Arab League	

And so there should be one constitution comprising of judiciary, executive and legislation and one civil law governing the whole of the humanity and all the nations of the world. The *Universal Code of Conduct* is one such and this Charter of *the World Union* is the second one.

'This World Union' is highly powerful and the enlightened men of the world will be alone at the helm of the organization, and hence, they impart justice and will run the world on the righteous path with peace, progress and prosperity besides safety and security. When all nations form this union called "the World Union," which is all powerful, all nations will get absolute freedom and liberty, because it is - *by the nations, of the nations, and for the nations.*

Even the power of nature cannot forbid the evolution of "One World" in due course, which once is a utopian concept, which now turned out to be a perfect reality. There is no other force in the world that objects or hinders the outcome of such a world system.

In fact, the human race as a whole is a 'peace loving' and 'peace living' and Dante remarked that, "the advancement of man, as the common goal of mankind." For, some all sorts of violence will come to an end in all times and in whole of the world. All fanatics will be subjugated and instead the universal and perfect peace keeping systems will develop at all levels. Then the welfare world will be established round the globe. In fact everybody, everywhere can perform as he pleases, as long as it doesn't cease the others' interests and intents, which are harmful to the society. Hence a most perfect and powerful organization must emerge for establishing a welfare world, but if it is weak and defective its fate will be that of 'the League of Nations, 'UNO' or the great Roman Empire. This global organization will have monopoly on the whole weaponry, all military forces and all sophisticated weapons of mass destruction like nuclear weapons, biological weapons. This world organization should be financially sound and be capable of meeting any calamities, came out naturally like earth quakes or floods, torrential rains or man-made like wars, other riots, calamities and many other such eventualities anywhere in the world.

But even for the formation of such world union many objections and obstruction may be there, as in the case of 'The League' or in the case of UNO. But now the whole world is in transition and such tendencies can be overcome at ease. Let us have discussion of a few of them.

1. The ideological differences may count on, in such formation of a world organization. People with some ideology may pressurize all people of the world through this organization to follow their own ideology. Then conflicts may arise in the organizational set up, which should be carefully dealt with. The conscience of the people is to be carefully considered. And it should also be approved in the General Council with the required majority. In the new ideologies, faiths, tenets and beliefs detrimental to the welfare society should be deleted vehemently.

2. Highly rich and advanced countries may object the formation of the 'World Union' with the apprehensions of losing their dominance in all aspects in the world scenario. But they can be well convinced that to be of equal status is of great value like brothers young and elder to live in one family together, which will be beneficial to all nations and the world. The 'World Union' is nothing but "The World Union" is- by the nations, of the nations, and for the nations". So the world political power will be vested in the super world power, which will promote revolutionized power of justice and equality all over the globe.

3. The other way the much lagging and the poor countries may object the very formation and joining of such 'The World Union' with the apprehensions of exploitation and domination or belittling the poorer nations amidst those sophisticated and advanced countries. The motto of the World Union is "Unite All nations of the world", and so such apprehensions need not be entertained.

4. The conflict between communism and capitalism may count on the formation of such world union as these are two distinct parallel channels with entirely opposite views.
They can be convinced for there is universal code of conduct of the nationals and nations, in that all will be involved and such system all differences will be nullified.

5. Countries having veto power will naturally in opposition for the formation of such world union and with the apprehension of losing their extra-ordinary power within this new union. But in such new world union, no veto power is needed as more powerful system of people's consensus will be introduced. All nations will have equal voice with consensus vote of the nationals. No such feelings need be entertained by those nations.

6. Some radical nations or nationals may vehemently oppose such formation of a new world body for their own selfish, meanest motives without any rational thinking. As in the case of UNO, and League of nations, there were such oppositions, they will be well convinced carefully propounding world over benefits out of such world body. It is usual of such opposition, but they can be well moved into the positive directions by rational arguments.
In the nature there will be opposition for opposition sake. But it can be subjugated by the rest of the society if such undue oppositions creep up to establish a good society.

7. The UNO may itself oppose the present formation of this new "The New World Union", feeling that it may be superfluous in the present day society. But all those objection may be over come as their goals and aims are different and distinct as the UNO 's prime goal is for establishing war free world and this TWU is for universal solidarity and friendship for the development and growth of the world, with mutual cooperation, coordination, and collaboration.
UNO is for war free world with universal peace where as TWU is for universal solidarity and mutual help and friendship and for the integration of the world and the advancement of all nations with mutual help.

8. When time ripens both the unions namely the UNO and TWU may merge into one union and can work together with a single goal of international development together as the goal of the farmer union will be outdated and no more needed. It is a welcome aspect for the world because it works out more effectively and efficiently with collective responsibilities, with the involvement of a number of states in the world. Facilities and workforce and burden of expenses will be well shared by all the nations proportionately.

9. One imminent danger may be the world violence may easily erupt, which can be controlled with meticulous care of this world body very powerfully with the measures as-the needs of the nations are being fulfilled,

the complaints of the nations are heeded, the conflicts between nations resolved amicably, all confrontations subjugated tactfully by having treaties and negotiations; and mutual discussions.

There is a contrast between the law of a lion and law of a lamb. Such a situation may prevail in the union. But as the motto is the unity of all nations of the world, such fears need not be felt by any individual nation in the union as there is balance of power and equilibrium maintained carefully.

Justice is more important than of all in the society whether in a nation or in a world. There is the law of natural justice one has to follow at all times by every national and by every nation in the world. There is a saying in Latin that

Fiat Justition et pereat mundus.
Justice be done even if the world should perish

In this process of creative evolution human beings are in transformation acquiring more and more agreeable and justifiable practices and good traits, and shedding all other bad traits. In the ladder of evolution, they may be well and they may be advanced well, another higher and superior species may rise to higher rung, the ultimate goal of mankind that is the advent of Humano divino[3]. In fact the nature of man is un-understandable a cosmic phenomenon. The law of nature, the nature of man, and the nature of the society and the world are to be well realized to unravel that very secret of that intriguing cosmic phenomenon.

This 'the World Union' and its legal system should be universally acceptable. The UNO is more viable than The League of Nations, but still it is weak for the task it has been assigned to in the world and thus, a need for the new world body aroused. The other way for the unification of the world-the foundation for one world system had already been laid in the other way technological and telecommunication wise, it has already been united and by global practices like in trade and business, scientific investigations and higher and international education the world is mingling and merging and the whole world shrank into a miniature world and politically it is distained to be in the offing. In the lore it was contemplated that east and west will never meet, which has been proved false and now not only east and west but also all nations are coming together.

Behai's a universalistic and a rationalized cult, which has grown out of 'Islam' is now superseding almost all ideologies, theologies, cults, and religions in the world, and occupying the second position after Christianity in the whole of the world.

Volumes of your good work may not be rewarding to you but it may be good to this world. So follow good path of life such that welfare world may come into its being. Population, once upon a time was a burden to any nation but now it became the wealth of the nation. Land is a wealth of a nation even if it barren and unfertile that can be used in many ways. Similarly skilled, and unskilled, intelligentsia un-intelligentsia are all usable for any nation.

One can do anything and anywhere in the world provided it is not harmful to anyone's interests Exploitation at any place, at any time, and at any levels should be curtailed at all levels and by all means and be justifiable, and non-corruptible.

Corruption is rampant in some countries, which is the biggest hurdle for their progress and prosperity hence, it should be totally curtailed by all means inevitably.

Men with corrupt practices cannot contribute anything to the society but exploit much the society and its innovations. Man's progressive endeavor alone that builds a welfare society and hence the world better.

In the long suffering of the society for centuries now an apt transition is taking place the world over in all aspects molding as a universal union or rather the world union, with such a power to make maximum good to the whole of the world in the lines of peace, justice, progress and prosperity and development, which is well conceivable without any exploitation at any levels anywhere either national or international levels.

In this changing shape of the power, as mentioned in the *universal code of conduct*, for all nationals and nations as well and as per the charter of the world union, it should be the mission of each and every nation in the world:

1. To strictly adhere to principles of democracy at all levels both in the national bodies and international bodies governmental and non-governmental.
2. To maintain peace and tranquility both at home and abroad with congenial environment in all aspects ethically and politically.
3. To be justifiable in all human activity and to do justice at all times.
4. To practice justifiable administration with ethical values by all sovereignties
5. Equality of justice should be shown in all aspects of discrimination, at all times in all nations of the world.
6. The discriminating aspects like advantageous and disadvantageous countries; racial, ideological and ethical differences, distinct social habits, languages, religion, and regions should be dealt with carefully and should be curtailed of in the society.
7. All governments should be strictly democratic with parliamentary practices, following the written constitution and elected members of the parliamentary body.
8. This 'The World Union' will naturally integrate with UNO in due course of time as shortly as possible and then a best world society will emerge.

This World Union will work in close connotation with United Nations Organization, and other global bodies for the present to achieve the single goal of establishing peaceful world with unity, universal solidarity and brotherhood, with mutual collaboration and cooperation. Each country will preserve its integrity, identity and ideology undisturbed, but besides extending its collaborative hand to the other countries and the world as well. But every country has to pledge that it will never wage a war against any other country and if any conflict that will arise will get resolved by peaceful negotiations and by approaching the hierarchy. It will maintain peace and solidarity amidst the countries of its region, continent and the world at large. The UNO was established to create war free world and the World Union prime aim is to establish and strengthen sociable and friendly relations between nations and continents and to promote strongly one world system and organize, and then the world will develop with congenial environment sharing fortunes and responsibilities; duties and commitments; resources and productions; scientific inventions, technological innovations and industrial advancements without any reservations.

The six continental unions will have the highest say in the administration of this World Union one of the continental just past head will head the World Union for four year term. He will be chosen in turns. And the structure of the World Union will be as shown below:

Table 8.2

The World Union Director General							
Administrative Structure **Secretary General**							
The Divisions in the Framework of the World Union							
Division 1 Administration & Personnel Secretary	**Division 2** Security & Military Secretary	**Division 3** Emergency Services Secretary	**Division 4** Academic Services Secretary	**Division 5** Medical Services Secretary	**Division 6** Science and Technology Secretary	**Division 7** Research & Industry Secretary	**Division 8** Religions & Humanity Services Secretary
		The	**Six**	**Continental**	**Unions**		
North American Continental Union NACU Deputy Director General	**South American Continental Union** SACU Deputy Director General	**African Continental Union** AfCU Deputy Director General	**European Continental Union** ECU Deputy Director General	**Asian Continental Union** AsCU Deputy Director General	**Australia & New Zealand Continental Union ANCU** Deputy Director General	**Arctic Region Belongs to the world** none but under the control of the World Union	**Antarctic Region Belongs to the world** none but under the control of the World Union
	Inter	**Continental**	**Regional** unions	can also be	formed		
		The	**Sub**	**Continental**	**Regions**		
NACU **Region 1** Director	**SACU** **Region 1** Director	**AFCU** **Region 1** Director	**ECU** **Region 1** Director	**ASCU Region 1** Director	**ANCU** **Region 1** Director		
NACU **Region 2** Director	**SACU** **Region 2** Director	**AfCU** **Region 2** Director	**ECU** **Region 2** Director	**AsCU Region 2** Director	**ANCU** **Region 2** Director		
NACU **Region 3** Director	**SACU** **Region 3** Director	**AfCU** **Region 3** Director	**ECU** **Region 3** Director	**AsCU Region 3** Director	**ANCU** **Region 3** Director		
NACU **Region 4** Director	**SACU** **Region 4** Director	**AfCU** **Region 4** Director	**ECU** **Region 4** Director	**AsCU Region 4** Director	**ANCU** **Region 4** Director		
NACU **Region 5** Director	**SACU** **Region 5** Director	**AfCU** **Region 5** Director	**ECU** **Region 5** Director	**AsCU Region 5** Director	**ANCU** **Region 5** Director		
Inter-Regional Unions	**Inter-Regional Unions**	**Inter-Regional**	**Inter-Regional**	**Inter-Regional Unions**	**Inter-Regional Unions**		

		Unions	Unions				
Among the 5 Regions any two or more can form an inter-regional union	Among the 5 Regions any two or more can form an inter-regional union	Among the 5 Regions any two or more can form an inter-regional union	Among the 5 Regions any two or more can form an inter-regional union	Among the 5 Regions any two or more can form an inter-regional union	Among the 5 Regions any two or more can form an inter-regional union		

The respective regions will be defined suitably and their HQ may be conveniently chosen with the necessary staff. Then all countries will be entangled with commitment and responsibility. This has to take place shortly such that the united world will be destined to emerge. The World Union will be with its Headquarter at the new township to be built called the Universe as mentioned earlier. In lieu of numerous other unions, associations or organizations, this world set up is the most convenient and congenial for the development of the whole world.

This Universal Township, which is unique of its kind, emitting the beams of enlightenment into the whole world and idealistic city-state in United States of America, far superior to that of Vatican City consisting of four units for the future world of peace and delight is to be built up.

The Road Map for the formation of the World Union

First of all a film is to be produced regarding the world and its evolutionary development as given in the works of R.N.Mohan namely 1. Mind a Miracle: Man Magnificent (Page Publishers, New York), Humano Divino (Page Publishers, New York), The Turning Points, in the lives of the Individuals, and in the histories of the nations and the world (Page Publishers, New York), and the Charter of the World Union (Creativespace) and thus, to be propagated well this concept of the Union around the globe.

Table 8.3.

S.No	Nature of the meeting	Countries likely to be participated	Agenda
1.	After Initial telephone consultations Informal and initial meeting	USA, UK, France, Japan, Germany, Brazil, Russia, India, China, South Africa	Initial discussions regarding the formation of the World Union. Core Committee to be designated.
2.	Core Committee	USA, UK, France, Japan, Germany, Brazil, Russian Federation, India, China, South Africa, Italy, Norway, Poland, Sweden, Denmark, Switzerland, and Australia	The first Core Committee of the World This committee will meet, which will discuss the feasibility of the formation of the Union. Continental unions will be designated.
3.	Continental Meetings	All countries of the concerned continents In North America, South America, Africa, Europe, Asia, Australia	Formation of continental unions will be made and designation of the regional unions of each continent
4.	Regional Meetings	The region unions will be formed in each continent	Region unions will be formed and commence the work of the World Union at the basic level
5.	The general meeting of the union	Heads of the states of all countries in the world	Preparation of the constitution and its adaption.
6.	General Body Meeting	Heads of all states Members Oath, Then formation of various councils, and officialdom	Fund rising, infrastructures of the HQ of TWU and various other continental and Regional unions. Assignment of plan of each building and campuses in the similar models uniformly to the suitable companies.
7	Inaugural Function	Heads of states of all countries in the world	*inauguration of the World Union*

In the subsequent meetings at the main HQ and Continental HQs while strengthening the union all development activities of the various countries will be planned and executed.

In the main HQ the Universe will be built as follows.

i. **Universe: The Divine:** Consists of the temples of all religions of the world- Christianity, Hinduism, Islam, Buddhism, Confucianism, Zoroastrianism and Baha'i and so on in the same campus, involving the world heads of all religions. It will be a distinctive religious set up in the whole world, which works to ease out all religious fanaticisms and ideological differences the world over and to build unity in diversity. This distinct and unique organization will help build world amity highly. The United States of America alone has potential to establish this. That will be a high research oriented religious set up in the world that never existed so far. This religious set up will work for the common good of all people and bring out the best from each religion and propagate, subtlest and conflicting concepts should not be touched if at all any.

ii. **Universe: The Enlightenment:** Consists of the World University and the Headquarters of United World Educational Organization (UWEO) comprising of the world educational institutes and a highly modern university involving all the stalwarts of the world in almost all fields of human intellectual activity. It is also a unique educational set up of the world. It should be the first of its kind in the whole of the world superseding Harvard, Princeton, Oxford and Cambridge. The world renowned people will have the placement here. The men trained here will have broad vision and different concept of life for the welfare of the whole humanity. Everyone belonging to these organizations thinks in terms of the world welfare. It will prepare the world leaders of tomorrow, with highest foresight and vision with world peace where all nations coexist by ending all conflicts and differences by negotiations and treaties. It will be the greatest organization on the face of the earth promoting research and in-depth study about all problems of the world. All institutions and universities accredited by UWEO should follow the concept of world vision as directed by it.

iii. **Universe**: **The World Union** will be having its Headquarters in this new city-state along with the six continental offices and offices for the two Polar Regions.

iv. **Universe: The Abode:** Consists of the residences of all people of supreme status and the concerned to the project and other required residences, facilities including the best modern medical research hospital, new educational facilities and modern shopping complex and so on. The world renowned scholars in all most all fields from science to spiritualism will be visiting the place and live and extend their knowledge to all the people of the world.

There will be a powerful TV Channel and the programs of this Universe will be on air always.

The whole campus should be an individual township located in USA in a most congenial place like Florida or California as in these states there exist needed land areas suitable for the purpose or any other country where suitable facilities are available.

The idea of World government had been contemplated for centuries, and some unauthorized organizations and institutions are just promoting this concept came into their being, and working and many of them have been already mentioned in the above pages. This institution has yet to form with its own worldwide military, executive, judiciary, and legislative bodies with more authority and power to govern the whole world and its independent states. For more details regarding the existing organization refer to http://en.wikipedia.org/wiki/World_government.

Now all men in the world will evolve to be pure, pious and perfect, with all righteousness and nobility, and thus emerge as universal being, or divine man and the whole world will be transformed and reformed into united word breaking barriers of all boundaries of the concerned country and all the countries in a continent will be united with cooperation and collaboration with all amity and friendship, and with strong ties with 'the World Union.' All citizens of the world will feel the one-world system under this 'World Union'. The entire world will develop with unity and friendship. And thus, the whole world will be reformed.

Besides the whole humanity will be transformed with endowed divinity and then super civilization will dawn. One should be pleasant and tranquil and speak softly and politely. The welfare world of peace and tranquility will come into its being by the occurrence of two sublime things-the first is for the whole of the humanity-that is the evolvement of *Humano divino*[iii] i.e. the Divine man and the second is for the entire world-that is emergence of "The World Union," which comprises of all countries of the world, without departing from their independence and sovereignty.

The transformation of the whole of the mankind-the present political, social, cultural, and economic aspects should be changed in an appropriate way, such that the individualistic and intergroup differences should be minimized, or rather nullified; the modern renaissance should start anew. All ideological differences and religious intolerance should come to an end and men should rise to the level of honoring every religion, every ideology and every individual with equanimity. All the men and all the nations of the world should follow the '*Universal Code of Conduct*' inexorably.

In fact for millions of years the humanity struggled and suffered and for centuries the mankind was in terror-stricken with enumerable internal wars and external threats and invasions, and for decades the men were in the troubles of economic depressions, worldwide. And of late at the beginning of the twenty-first century the whole world and the whole of humanity are anxiously looking for peace, progress and prosperity and aspiring to bring a new civilization-a new era-*the era of intelligence*- the *era of friendship, mutual cooperation, mutual collaboration and mutual help.* If avoiding all conflicts is one aspect, building up amity and serene and congenial environment is the other aspect, between men or nations and these two aspects run in parallel channels inter-related and interdependent.

There are different regimes namely-monarchic, aristocratic, autocratic, tyrannical, dictatorial, totalitarian, fascistic, feudalism, and so on and amidst all these the democracy is considered to be the best as it is defined as- it is by the people, of the people, and for the people. This republic and democratic system alone ensures peace, progress and prosperity, avoiding all sorts of conflicts and confrontations. But this democracy should be genuine involving truly all men in the concerned society, without any corruptive or coercive practices, and should not be an oligarchy. Now wonderfully, in the present twenty-first century almost all countries in the world transformed to democratic systems of governance.

The people of any country always wish peace, progress and prosperity, and in these democratic systems it is possible, whereas the country's fate totally depends on the whims and fancies of the men at the helm without anybody's objection in the other systems like that of monarchism or dictatorial system and the civilians will be the maximum sufferers.

For centuries, with struggle and strife, with wars and aggressions, with oppressions and suppressions, and with forcible occupations and with all exploitations, the whole world moved on, and at last the universal devastation occurred on the planet. And then the concept of one world system developed. With the conflicts of numerous ideological differences and the resulting controversies and confrontations, the universal code of conduct for all nations and for all nationals of the world became inevitable. Consequently, one frontier of all nations, one class of law for all citizens of the world, leading to one political, social, and economic system is ushering in around the globe. The very stratum of the present day society has encapsulated with knowledge and enlightenment and hence the progress and advancement became certain.

Around the world all the problematic issues within its boundaries are being settled amicably by every nation, the exploitation of one individual by another individual; one society by another society; and one nation by another nation disappeared with just some exceptions. Once the population was a burden for the nation but now it became the prime wealth of the nation.

In various stages of the development of the society, many transformations are taking place, the concepts and the ideologies and the very thought process of the people are being changed. The universal reformation is rapidly going on. Consequently, the development of every nation and hence the development of the whole world became imminent.

None can go against the eternal laws of nature, and the rational reasoning. The commanding concepts of the present day world are entirely different to that of the earlier. There are eternal truths such as freedom, liberty and justice, which are common to all citizens in the world and to all nations of the world. Even the communism abolishes superstitious religious dogmas and wishes to constitute a new universal code instead.

In the present day instead of piecemeal society of nations of the world with different groups like- developed and under-developed; advantageous and disadvantageous; and well-advanced and ill-advanced, we will have a conglomeration of all nations of the world in which the free development of each nation will be highly promoted with all needed assistance from around the globe, and thus, free development of the whole world will result in. This new universal concept developed with all the experiences of the past and in view of the planning ahead for the future of the world.

In the countries where modern civilization has been fully developed, a new class of nations may build up. But all other countries, which are lagging behind will be assisted to build up themselves, to become the best possible state of the society and the best possible state of the world and then they proclaim the harmony of the society and harmony of the world as well.

In fact the very interest of human nature is to be happy and comfortable and this advancement of the world will satisfy that interest by all means.

In this new world order many drastic changes can be brought in. To quote a few of them-

1. All over the world collective farming may be introduced instead of individual farming, avoiding individual farmers' losses and then the farmers round the globe will be happy.
2. Agriculture and industry are to be closely associated and the collective work through industries to be promoted.

3. The farmers and consumers are to be closely associated in agricultural produce, avoiding all middlemen, benefitting actual producers.
4. Transportation and communication may be nationalized bringing only one system through-out the nation, and linking all systems of the world.
5. Medical aid should be free in all nations of the world, revamping the very medical systems, avoiding all exploitations in the field.
6. All financial institutions should be nationalized and no private financial transactions and thus, the exploitations in this sector may be nullified.
7. The education from primary school to the university level should be made free or at the best on loan basis at the higher levels.
8. More perfect formula for taxation may be brought in.
9. Scope for working to every able man, whatever may it be, just for the society and thus, for the country as well.

This universal conglomeration of nations will satisfy the motto-

Unite, all nations of the world; Unite, the whole humanity of the world.

In fact, if we consider the human history from 600 BC to 2000 AD the whole world as said earlier, was in turmoil of bloody wars national and international, riots and civil wars, There is significant transformation in the world that almost all nations turned to be democratic or with elected parliaments, and the war mongering attitudes subsided amidst nations one-way and there is change in human nature as well, as all the mankind became more responsible and concerned for the welfare world. For these purposes numerous proposals are in the air for example, One World Government, The World Federation. Monroe Doctrine propounded these types of concepts, following that the League of Nations saw the light in the past decades just after the First World War, with the initiation of Woodrow Wilson, the then President of United States of America. But unluckily it was not successful. And of late superseding it the United Nations Organization (UNO) came into its being binding all nations of the world. But this UNO has its own failures and contradictions, because some unequal status is prevailing much between the member nations of the Organization. The Veto power at times was a hurdle in the administration of justice hampering the equality status. Consequently, a newer Organization has yet to come superseding this UNO with more power and international status involving all countries of the world with equal status and thus, "The World Union", for which foundations were being laid already.

Table 8.4. The contrast of the UNO and the World Union

United Nations Organization and other World Institutions/ organizations	The World Union
1. The prime goal of UNO is to control wars and to establish peace in the world.	1. The prime goal of the union is to promote good and friendly relations among all nations with mutual cooperation and collaboration, mutual help and developing congenial and serene environment the world over with amity and universal solidarity and brotherhood, and thus, to establish prosperous, harmonious and progressive world.
2. The voting system of the member-states promotes inequality.	2. All member states have equal rights of voting.
3. Population of the concerned country is not considered but other aspects economic and political are considered	3. The population, politico-economic and social aspects will be well considered
4. It is not a world government and hence could neither enact nor enforce laws.	4. As it is the union- *by the nations, of the nations and for the nations*, it can be empowered to enact and enforce the law, binding all nations of the world.
5. It is only having some advisory position to some sovereign states.	5. It is as a legal body will be-not only in advisory position but also will be in authoritative position, and if need be, majority opinion will prevail without any veto power for any nation. Sometimes the power of the vote with the strength of the population of the nation may also be considered.
6. It has no military, police or any other force of its own. Expect peacekeeping forces with the support of the solely some nations.	6. It will have its own military, police, security and investigative forces with the support of all nations' fund.
7. It depends on the generosity of the member-states funding and financial support.	7. It is mandatory for the member-states to pay membership dues as fixed by the Union taking into consideration- the economic status of the concerned country.
8. All its decisions are not binding on all member-states. It varies	8. All the decisions if once ratified in the Union are totally binding without any variation And all member-states should follow those rules invariably.
9. It is not powerful to enforce any principle however good may it be.	9. It is so empowered and hence can enforce any principle that was approved in the union
10. It cannot do anything to an erring state.	10. It can act suitably on the erring state. For example, the country's sovereignty can be taken out and union will rein for some time and build democratic system again with the consensus of the people concerned.
11. It is unable to resolve any conflicts national or international.	11. It will be so empowered to resolve any conflicts national or international of any country and the Union's verdict is final on the concerned nation.
12. Its negotiations are not well considered by the erring nations	12. Its negotiations and treaties have to be well-honored by all the member-nations and if need be Union is empowered to strongly enforce without fail. It is binding on all member-nations.
13. It failed to establish universal peace and can neither avoid nor control war and warfare in the world.	13. It will be so empowered such that it will establish universal peace in the entire world and can avoid and totally control all types of wars national and international.
14. It could not bring any radical changes in the world.	14. It will be empowered to bring radical changes in the world.

15. It could not actively interfere in all international problems and conflicts and could not solve them efficiently.	15.It will take prime role in solving all world problems and can enforce the decision efficiently with possible action on the erring nation
16.It could not fulfill its great mission of bringing social, cultural, political, and economic changes in the world well	16. It is well empowered to bring the needed economic, social, political and cultural changes in all nations of the world
17. In no world body including UNO has the power or responsibility of shouldering and resolving the international conflicts efficiently and perfectly. Hence whenever they arise there is every possibility of erupting any war	17. After the advent of the World Union, resolving all world conflicts will be the sole responsibility of the Union and hence, no scope of erupting wars, instead the "Universal Solidarity and brotherhood" will be highly promoted.
The World Government	**The World Union**
1. If it is World Government-the national sovereignty and its independence will be shattered.	1. In the World Union-all the sovereign states will be the members of the Union and their independence and sovereignty will be well preserved with some rare exceptions if it becomes so inevitable but soon will it be restored with the consensus of the people..
2. It will promote economic, social and political development of the member-states.	2. It not only develops economic, social, political and cultural aspects but promotes mutual cooperation, mutual coordination, and collaboration, amity and friendship amidst all nations of the world.
3. Some countries may assume dominant role and that leads to differences and finally to wars.	3. No need of domination of any country, but all countries will be on equal footing, but in congenial, amicable, and friendly environment with mutual help and economically, politically and culturally all nations will survive happily.
4. Some of the sovereign states are war mongering for economic and political reasons, and thus, peace has been hampered. And UNO assumed spectator status.	4. Such tyrannical or dominating situations do not arise as there will be neither economic disparities nor political differences. Each country will stick on its own boundaries and think of cooperating with its neighbors and others as well. Universal solidarity exists.
5. The world Government may be concerned with governance only and hence at times the sovereignty of any nation may affect.	5. As mutual cooperation and collaboration will be highly developed there will be no need of affecting the sovereignty of any nation at any time with rare exceptions of erring nations.
6. Finally for establishing the world of peace and tranquility either UNO or the World Government is not the sufficient means and so some other means is needed modifying all the existing defects.	7. Finally the establishment of the World Union will be inevitable as a world democratic system as it will be- *by the nations, of the nations and for the nations of the world.* This will supersede the other world organizations existing.

There are around 196 member-states in UNO and we can as well include the other nations like Taiwan, Vatican City and some such other nations, which are not members of United Nations Organization into 'The World Union,' and each head of the state has one vote and the strength of the vote may be fixed with the population of that state whenever needed when consensus of the people has to be obtained. This 'World Union' will work for the survival of the humanity with peace and tranquility with mutual cooperation and mutual collaboration in congenial, amicable and friendly environment with the sole aim of building up universal solidarity and brotherhood; and innovation and growth.

Equality is of utmost importance of human life, which has distinct dimensions and amongst them the foremost aspect is economic equality-the rich and the poor. The conflict between these two classes of the rich and the poor exists since time immemorial. The economic freedom resulted in, enormous growth in all dimensions, like scientific and technological innovations, industrial developments, and then the free enterprise all over the world, and consequently, the international trade practices, that boost up the morale and liberty around the globe. But un-necessary competition and undue exploitation should be curtailed at all levels and in all regions. There are numerous types of economies namely-wartime economy, communist economy, socialistic economy, fascist economy, feudal economy, and Nazi economy, and so on, which are all good in their own way, theoretically glossy, but practically they are all unsuccessful, bringing tremendous hardship to the citizens of the concerned society/country. These types of economies prevailed during the times when there was no respect to the human life and individual liberty in the country may be during the wartime or tyrannical regime was on the run.

The political evolution in the past few centuries resulted in, transforming all types of government systems, socialism and democracy succeeded monarchism, communism then that was superseded by the responsible democratic systems, which is triumphant in almost all countries in the world and consequently, all of them collectively are developing the whole world. This is leading to the era of perpetual peace all over the world. Simultaneously, all economic systems all over the world, national wide and international wide are also being modified.

Even in the evolution of economic systems the world over, resulting in, the democratic system of governance of corporations and industrial systems, cooperative societies, certain community or group societies or nationalized organizations leading to mass production and huge corporations and all of which have been controlled by a group of directors working on democratic basis to be elected for fixed terms only. Thus, the culture of capitalism did many good things bringing growth and progress for the country and for the whole world as well.

Education including science and technology play important roles in building up a peaceful world, because it gives knowledge and wisdom and broad world vision. If all the inventions are well utilized for the benefit of mankind-instead of utilizing them for any destructive purpose that will result in immeasurable suffering to the whole humanity-then the whole world will be happy and tranquil. So education should be, instead of regional or national-the universal education[2] with world concept that should be imparted. For this a world organization namely- "The United World Educational Organization[2]," should be established, which has been already discussed. The nineteenth and twentieth centuries are highly significant in the history of humanity as scientific, technological and industrial innovations were and are being at the peak and number of wars that occurred during these times was also high. For example, the two great world wars occurred in twentieth century only when the world was advancing scientifically very fast.

So, perfectly right universal education[2] should be imparted at all levels in all countries of the world, which will develop human commitment and human responsibilities for the world leading to peace, progress and prosperity of the world.

All religions in the world preach the same law of love for the humanity, which can promote the end of all wars in the world. Because, when all religions equally respected and all ideological differences subdued that bring peace and tranquility and the question of conflict does not arise at all. Instead, it results in ever lasting peace all over the world. In fact superstition and ignorance reign supreme all over the society and the rules and regulations cannot be enforced on such ignorant masses unless all of them will become well educated and knowledgeable. So the two vital aspects the education and the religion are to be well addressed for the sake of welfare world and for establishing universal peace all over the world and bringing supreme development and welfare to the world.

As religion is the binding force for the humanity and so we have to address this aspect as well. For all religions "The Universal Religious Order", amalgamating almost all the concepts from all world religions will be formulated. If there are conflicting concepts-all the concepts will be incorporated in it intelligently without promoting any differences. For example, what the Ten Commandments of Jesus Christ, the Manusmruthi's ten-fold path of life and Buddha's ten-fold path and Confucius's concepts of life are all same, enunciating the same path of life almost similarly. And hence, this "The Universal Code of Conduct," has to be adapted by all men and all nations in the world.

Another aspect is education at all levels. The "United World Educational Organization[2]," will be established, which will promote the concept of the universal solidarity and brotherhood at all levels from school to university all over the world, which will change the world scenario. Education will be revamped with newer concepts and people learn respecting all religions and races; countries and cultures; and learn to minimize their economic disparities and sociological differences.   And thus, the humanity will be reformed to the best possible way for developing universal harmony.

And for other political aspects "The World Union" will be established, which will act as a powerful binding force of all nations in the world, building up universal amity and solidarity with the ties of friendship of all people in the world. And thus, the world will be reconstructed for this purpose and goal.

In fact, the concept of conquering the world waned away. Almost all rivalries between the nations ended. There exists none who wish to become an emperor, or planning to invade any other nation or to occupy the land of others in the present day world. But all people are aspiring international peace and progress instead of their own nation solely. And people transformed to the concepts of altruism-cooperation and coordination and with love and sympathy toward the fellow human beings became the decisive factors of the contemporary world, because of the right universal education[2] and the social, cultural and transformations in the society. Consequently, all social differences and political conflicts miraculously disappeared in the society, and that is leading to the happy and harmonious, prosperous and peaceful world of tomorrow.

In fact, for the very survival of the human society, the members of the society should possess the altruistic nature and the world is moving with those men of altruism only. Instead, if there is egoistic tendency only that predominates, then the existence of the society will be questionable; as egocentric nature promotes unending conflicts leading to catastrophic end of the society.

The chariot of the human society moves on the wheels of compassion, consideration, love, fairness, and sympathy. Then there exists serene and congenial environment and people live happily with mutual cooperation and coordination with concern with each other. People with such altruistic nature will be very friendly and amicable; kind and considerate; loyal and compassionate; and show respect and reverence and devoted with adoration towards the other fellow beings. If the society consists of men of such nature then how great that society will be?

Lord Jesus Christ, Lord Gautama Buddha, and in the recent past Mahatma Gandhi, Nelson Mandela were all of altruistic natured people. This altruistic nature in man helps him to realize his divine nature, and thus, transforming him as man divine or *Humano divino*[iii]. Those men divine work for the welfare of humanity, whatever may be their field, they contribute greatly to the world. The highest achievers in science and technology; religion and spiritualism; fine arts and aesthetics; social or political; culture, music or literature are all of altruistic natured people only.

In fact, this divine nature is inherent biologically in every living being and so in man as well. But man alone is capable of harnessing it out. These altruistic natured divine men can visualize well the world phenomenon, and hence, discourage or even nullify all inter-racial conflicts and inter-religious friction and establish peaceful and harmonious world. They are capable of transforming socio-cultural system and can establish creative solidarity between individuals, groups, nations and in the whole world. They also bring suitable modifications in using the scientific and technological innovations, cultural and religious systems, moral and ethical values, by being at the helm in the society with their righteous attitudes and the nature of nobility. When once the political, social, economic and cultural systems are being modified by them into one universal system in which all religions will be honored, all races will be treated equally, and all human beings be given equal opportunity of life and living that will be the new civilization- the divine civilization.

The degraded humanity is to be uplifted to high moral conscience, with sublime social and cultural values in order to establish welfare world. The realization of divinity is destined to dawn on every human being inevitably. Centuries together what had been occurred is that-man degraded, and when moral self-degradation manifested on man all his cruel temperament developed to the brim, in him, resulting in, wars, riots, revolutions, and conflicts. And as an example, the two grievous world wars, and consequently, emancipation of millions of people (may be about 50 million people) the world over occurred.

In the confused and conflicting state of affairs as in the world till the recent past the universal law and the universal culture could not be imbibed in the people all these centuries, but now the time is ripened, advancement is going on in all spheres of human activity, and the evolutionary forces are leading both the humanity and the world to transcend into a well sophisticated stature. All such divine men are emerging with sublime thoughts and actions along with super-sensory, super-rational, and super-conscious aspects and the world, in its consequence, destined to be harmonious. The whole world will be of immeasurable happiness and much more noble men than ever before. The nature of those men will be universal, righteous, and so to say altruistic. And they lead the whole world to be highly creative, harmonious, peaceful and tranquil. In fact these men divine will be well-cultured, well-realized, and conscious and super conscious *Humano divinos*[2] who will develop universal values in the world. Then a new era will be ushered in. And the whole world will be the noblest and sublime that never existed, if not in the pre-historic period of the Indian sub-continent, or in Mayan civilization in Mesoamerica, or rather in pre-historic civilizations that existed in the remote worlds in the lore.

Sorokin[5] said that, ".. Thus will dawn an era in which man apprehends and controls the inorganic and the organic, achieves self-control, and penetrates even the super-organic realm. He will become tne nation of the highest creative forces of the universe, attuned to the Godhead. Deep peace of mind and goodwill toward one's fellows will prevail."

That is how he means a divine man's evolvement and the emergence of the harmonious world.

If not science and technology misused or abused, but if used for peaceful purposes, the world will grow further and further in almost in all dimensions. Sorokin[5] stresses the advent of new religion-the religion of love as- "love of man for his fellow men, for God, and for the entire universe; love manifests in deeds, as well as in words, and aspirations. It must be capable of lifting man again to the infinite heights of the Godhead and of reestablishing the broken unity between humanity and the creative soul of the cosmos. It must reassert the divine origin of man...."

He believed the divine nature of man and the upcoming of a harmonious world. He said further that, "It must inspire man with an unquenchable longing to transcend the subconscious and conscious phases of his personality in the quest of the subconscious realm of immortal truth, goodness and beauty."

These views expressed by Sorokin[5] confirms the advent of superman or man divine-Humano divino[4]-and its impact the world over generating powerful forces of love, peace and beauty. Besides mutual cooperation, coordination and mutual help the attitude of loving the other human being with equanimity should also be developed in all men in that newer society. Befitting to that new society, new laws will be enacted with high moral and ethical values preserving the natural law of universe in every aspect, superseding all the earlier confusing laws that were existing may be like British law, American law, Hindu law, Muslim law, Greek law or Roman law and so on. And thus, the universal system of law and ethics besides *the universal code of conduct* should be built in. That alone creates exalted humanity on the globe.

Fine arts and literature are also powerful forces for ennobling man and for promoting universal solidarity in the human kingdom and uplifting every man to the realms of sublime thoughts and supreme ideals.

For transformation of culture and for developing unity and solidarity in the world Sorokin[5] said that, "It becomes once more an enlightening, inspiring and ennobling force, unfolding a vision of divine beauty, purifying man by its author- and is tending to unite the whole humanity in a single intimate brotherhood."

These creative and noble divine men will develop a harmonious cultural order-that is the dawn of a new human culture with full of peace, harmony and happiness. Cooperative human relationship will prevail over the society. The egoism and demoralization that was developed all over the contemporary world will be diminished. During the past centuries numerous monarchies, dynasties, empires, regimes, aristocracies existed, each comprising some countries of the world, but the whole world was never united. It never came together in the whole history of the world. And some of the regimes could do well, congenial and constructive, but some others were disastrous and destructive. All they resulted in, enumerable wars, some were regional, some were national, some other were international and even intercontinental and finally, the world wars broke twice in the human history, which were highly devastating, with heavy loss of life and property all over the globe causing misery and suffering to the humanity. Besides so many civil wars, cold wars, conflicts occurred in many countries all over the world, for centuries together, but when all men became wise, intelligent and knowledgeable, competent and altruistic, things changed, efforts started for establishing war-free world, bringing peace on the globe. A few of these efforts partially successful and partially failed and that is leading to further those efforts not only for building peaceful world, but to build welfare world with universal solidarity with mutual cooperation and mutual coordination, and mutual help. That caused the emergence of "The World Union," all-powerful to building up the world well-being with the support and commitment of all sovereign, democratic nations of the world. This 'World Union' is so empowered to strip of the sovereignty of any erring nation, and rebuilt it as a democratic nation with the consensus of its citizens. The membership in 'the World Union' is open to all countries of the world that pledge stating that-Not to wage war and not to invade any other nation; maintain sovereign democratic republic; any conflict that arises between any two nations will be resolved only by peaceful negotiations or with the cooperation of 'the World Union' instead of confronting with the concerned nations. Every country should maintain amicable and friendly relations with all other countries and build universal solidarity in the world and express full support to 'the World Union' in all circumstances. All member nations should follow disarmament policies and should nullify all their destructive action of any type either terroristic or peace disturbing. No member-state should disrupt peace and tranquility of the people of any nation in the world. And lastly, all member-nations should follow constructive and creative path to build a better welfare world. Then the world will be highly livable and the gains the people get will be much more than one can imagine. 'The World Union' will have legislative, judiciary and executive bodies with different ambitions and goals. And it is a highly competent world body, with high moral and ethical values, that behaves impartially and justifiably, strictly following the universal law and will never play power politics with mean objectives. Besides having sovereignty, all the member states maintain sophisticated friendly relations with all other nations, and hence, free trade, travel and communications will be provided to all the people irrespective of their nationality, race and religion without any undue restrictions and controls.

'The World Union' will be a sovereign democratic organization with all nations of the world as its members and can be defined as- *by the nations, of the nations, and for the nations.* And so whenever needed, it should obtain consensus of all the people of the world through their leaders or heads of the states on the matters of importance for example, nonproliferation of nuclear weapons, controlling of terroristic activities, and industrial policies, and all such matters concerned to the nations and the world as well, then all nations involve united.

All power-mongering, corruptive, untrustworthy politicians should neither be elected nor be nominated in any responsible position at any level, as it will hamper the peace, progress and prosperity of the people. All dubious practices should be discouraged and democracies with such unethical men should not be promoted. All dictatorial, communistic, Nazi or tyrannical systems should be curtailed at all levels because they effect the freedom and liberty of the citizens and they cannot build welfare, peaceful societies. Peoples' non-friendly principles and policies all should be eliminated from the administration at all levels. For example, conspicuous economic policies will disrupt the tranquility of the society. But when the society develops and when people become well educated these disparities automatically become nullified. Equitable distribution of wealth all over the world will lead to improvement of the standard of living of the people, and hence, tranquility will be prevailed the world over. The people, all over the globe wish to have the world-free from all emergencies like wars- national or international, civil wars or cold wars, regional or racial wars, revolutions or riots, political disturbances, unrest of all types-social or political, economic disruptions, which are all man-made catastrophes; but wish to have peaceful and tranquil world, which is safe and secure, progressive and prosperous, where they can live happily.

And so, the reconstruction of the whole world besides the reformation of the humanity by revolutionizing all political, social, economic and cultural systems, and also, the educational system of the world is inevitable. Good education leads reformation of the minds of the people, and hence, his behavioral pattern will also change, and consequently, his character and conduct will be modified accordingly. In fact, it is highly impossible for a person to be altruistic, divine, righteous and noble in this vicious society of egoistic tendencies. But the newly evolving men-divine with super-sensory intelligence, with apt and logical reasoning, and super conscious intuition, can bring such beauty of peace and happiness into the streams of contemporary society certainly.

Optimistically, it is possible to develop affable human relations the world over, to prevent disastrous wars, riots and revolutions, and all types of conflicts and to build peaceful world by modifying the human beings with appropriate education and reorganizing socio-economic and political systems in the world, which these men divine will shoulder and will bring a welfare world. Because these divine men-within his conscious phase-his well-molded total personality-and by fully utilizing his conscious and super-conscious forces-by transforming himself-and can transform the society and the whole world as well in due course of time, leading to much more tranquil and happy, peaceful and prosperous world. In fact, when man's highest conscious and super conscious energies are well utilized then he will become highly creative and productive and his divine nature comes out into play in the world. Sorokin[5] exposes divinity in man as follows- "The super conscious energies and activities constitute the highest stratum of man's personality, representing the supreme type of creative functioning. They are frequently designated as the "divine in man, the manifestation of Godhead, the Creative genius" and so on."

And further Sorokin[5] stresses that, "What is needed is the concentration of humanity's efforts in unlocking the secret of super-conscious as the realms of the most powerful, most creative and most ennobling forces in the entire universe."

In all religious systems, whatever may it be, the main object of the human life is the union with the supreme. And it is all to achieve that super conscious state otherwise called divine-state. Then the man himself becomes man divine or rather *Humano divino[4]*.

As said earlier these men divine will be highly creative and will make epoch making inventions and discoveries in all most all fields of human intellectual activities. They will change the society, change the human culture, change man's thinking processes, his actions   and his behavioral patterns, and thus, consequently, change the whole world as well, in all dimensions. In fact, conscience, consciousness, super consciousness, and constructive forces of men that are all needed for the development of the world in all possible fields of intellectual activity. So all the progressive concepts that are in different fields that are being developed in different countries the world over will be well utilized and will be well propagated the world over by 'the World Union' that will help in building the welfare world. All these lead to the emergence of a new renaissance movement-a new culture, which will be a more prosperous period in the human history. That will be the road of renaissance for the whole of the world and period of transfiguration for the whole of humanity and to transform this world to be a happy world.

This 'World Union' is a new international system, which will promote a new international citizenship that will model the whole world as a welfare world. In fact for centuries the aspirations and demands of the peoples and nations the world over are to build another world system, which can bring 'universal solidarity' in the whole world. After the advent of men divine the peoples' mind will inevitably change and everyone will get a new drive to work well for the world and the time has ripened and it is going to bear fruition. The restructuring the whole world with regional wise, national wise, continental wise and global wise systems will be developed, having well-defined international norms, with the participation of all countries of the world, sharing responsibilities, and holding the duties assigned with the sole aim of building welfare world spreading the fabric of friendship the world over. As the interdependence will be well dealt with and international cooperation will be further strengthened, international collaboration will be well promoted, and thus, by establishing universal solidarity the world over that aspired welfare world will come into its being. Then the global future will be bright and prospering. Even though each country has its own sovereignty, its political system, its geography, its history, its economy, its social factors, its culture, and its races, which are all unique and distinct, but all these distinct countries will join into the main stream of the world community by accepting the prime principle-"Unity in Diversity." This World Union will be an amiable, liberal and powerful international organization/authority, which can serve well and command well if it is constrained to do so in case of need. There are some existing global powers namely- the United States of America, European Union and in the past Union of Soviet and Socialistic Republics. But now after the advent of this 'World Union' all such unilateral global powers will be amalgamated into the unique global power-'The World Union'. In fact there are upcoming global powers besides the above in the present twenty-first century namely-Peoples' Republic of China, India, Russia and Brazil along with these South Africa joined hands and consequently, the organization called BRICS came into existence, which can balance the future world scenario, by challenging the new world order of tomorrow, besides the present super powers. Even though the Muslim world had a different path in the social, political and economic development of the world, with entirely different concept of liberalism, and acting entirely in a distinct way to the rest of the world, it is the time to revive their view points for building up the welfare world and for the global common good.

One way the upheavals in the global economy, the drastic fluctuations in the oil prices the world over and depletion of oil resources, and radical ideological differences, some sort of political dominations and undue competitions in trade and commerce effecting the peace and tranquility, safety and security of the nations and the world, and so a healthy global community has to be build up inexorably. This emerging new global community will built, a sustainable, ever enduring and everlasting development the world over. 'The World Union,' the newly evolved global community, will have a virtuous world vision, noble perspective of the humanity, with high moral and ethical values, well-defined global norms, and maintain perfect law or order and provide seamless safety and security to the citizens around the globe. This Union, having high priorities for research and development in almost all fields will help the world to grow and innovate. In fact the world is making rapid strides economically and industrially, and the global stature is itself transforming fast. And it is further to be accelerated for building up the aspired welfare world. A potent global force is emerging with the united efforts of all nations of the world, and in fact, that will be this-"The World Union." It is inexorably desirable for the following reasons:

1. To develop universal solidarity and friendship amongst all nations and continents of the world. The sole aim of this Union is to bring all nations together for collective growth, innovation and development, without any undue competition.

2. To develop international, intercontinental cooperation, collaboration and coordination.

3. To promote sustainable development of the whole world, by involving all nations and territories either members or not, collectively.

4. To protect and preserve the independence and sovereignty of each and every nation of the world.

5. To help and assist the effected country due to any natural disasters immediately. The Union will be capable of shouldering this responsibility easily instead of by any individual country.

6. To be well-concerned with all global issues collectively by all nations, like global warming, depletion of oil resources, terroristic attacks, global economic depressions, pollution and ecological imbalances and so on.

7. To promote research and development in all most all fields for accelerating the entire world development at large.

8. To control totally the arms-race by the individual nations, as there will be no need of procuring and equipping them individually as safety and security is the responsibility of the World Union, and hence, it will come into action in any such case.

9. As no country need to wage a war against any other country, all those funds required for defense will be diverted to either for constructive purpose in the country or to 'the World Union,' which will shoulder the defense responsibility.

10. 'The World Union' will be so empowered and strengthened sufficiently politically, economically and even militaristic wise to face any eventualities boldly with competence, with the support of all countries.

11. To face all global challenges with competence like-global economy, global political and diplomatic issues, global peace, safety and security, global climatic changes and natural disasters like tsunamis, volcanic eruptions and earthquakes and so on.

12. To formulate global rules and regulations for safety and security, and for progress and prosperity.

13. To uplift weak and failing states in all possible dimensions, economic, educational, social, political and cultural.

14. To revive and rebuild the conflict-torn countries and societies whether they are regional, national, international or intercontinental because those conflicts affect the global system as well.

15. To promote and preserve democratic systems in all nations in the world.

After the advent of this 'World Union,' it will not be any one country or a few countries that will dominate the world, but all countries combined and collectively, they will participate in building up and developing the united world for its progress and prosperity; peace and security. Consequently, the global economy will develop the world over. Every country has to shoulder the responsibility of this global task of facing all global challenges, by formulating needed global systems and for fast transforming the world and to build greater cooperation, coordination and collaboration amongst all nations of the world. That will result in the 'Universal Solidarity and brotherhood' as well. So this global system must possess the needed well-sophisticated defense system with appropriate finance, military and weaponry.

'The World Union' will be so empowered and well-strengthened by all nations of the world with constructive leadership, and every nation should respect it, and the universal law of the Union will be binding on all member-states of the Union, and consistent cooperation and participation amongst all member nations should be there invariably without any disparities.

Wonderfully, the uni-polar and bi-polar world transformed to multi-polar world and that will be evolved to non-polar world as 'The World Union,' which will not either exert or exercise any such power politics, but instead it works with the united efforts for the advancement of all nations of the world. It will be a democratic universal system and for any global decisions, concerned to the welfare of the citizens, their consensus will be taken, either directly or through their leaders as their vote will be entangled with the strength of the population they represent.

As the times changed, voice of the people became so strong, now the evolution of an international system is imminent to tackle the new global issues that are creeping up, and all people of all nations are constrained to involve. And hence, the united world body is inevitably needed to promote and preserve peace and tranquility the world over.

The membership is open to all nations, but after giving an undertaking that-1. It will help to build 'universal solidarity' amongst all nations of the world, 2. It will not use force against any other nation even in the case of military aggression, 3. The total responsibility will be put on the shoulders of the Union to deal the situation to resolve it by peaceful negotiations and to draft a treaty of peace, and will be confirmed by the two involved parties and the Union's authority, 4. If a nation does not heed the advice of the Union in an odd situation, it will lose its sovereignty and Union will take the reins of the nation and re-establish democratic system by taking the consensus of its citizens, 5. The nation will built up and maintain friendly and amicable relations with every other nation. 6. Every nation should agree to follow these tenets unvaryingly.

So far the whole world's economy is being controlled by some pivotal world financial markets, and certain leaderships in trade, commerce and industry and some advanced countries of the world, but soon after the advent of 'the World Union' the world's economic perspective will be constrained to be changed. The global prosperity will not be affected with the economic upheavals thereafter as the whole world will be working in unison, and 'the World Union' will play pivotal role in all such crucial matters more diligently by establishing a well-defined global economic system. Fundamentally, no country need to strive for any global leadership in any field either political, or social, or economical, instead every country will strive for mutual cooperation, mutual friendship and mutual help with strong tie-ups in research, trade, industry and all other aspects.

Most importantly, global citizenship will be promoted. Every country should take responsibility for all global environmental changes like climate, ecological imbalances, and also political disturbances and work for the global wellbeing-its existence, its growth and its development. All countries should concentrate for the advancement of the globe and for the growth of the humanity and 'the World Union' will act as a catalyst and promote it.

How the world will be moving in the future? What will be the opinion of the mankind the world over, about the upcoming future? Will there be any individual or any nation aspiring to win over the world? These are worthy addressable questions that are lingering the author's mind that culminated in him to write this book.

We will propound a proposal even though ambitious but possible, as some foundations have already been laid and in some way certain aspects are in process as well. And now we have to further those aspects for the benefit of the citizens all over the world, for the benefit of community of nations of the world, or rather, for the benefit of the whole world as well-for peace, progress and prosperity, for safety and security and for the growth and development in all possible dimensions. Instead of bilateral, multilateral relationships that are prevailing in the contemporary world, through this World Union-a highly congenial and comfortable friendly relations will be built up, as every nation is aspiring for such an international relationship and that becomes highly feasible through this World Union, which is a greatly liberal, democratic global system, accessible to all nations- as said earlier it is -*"of the nations, by the nations and for the nations."*

In the past decades the "League of Nations and League of Democracies" came into light with some nations of the world, but they could not comprise all nations of the world. Even the United Nations Organization was established with lofty ideals befitting in those days decades ago, but it has its own numerous failures and incapacities, unsusceptible for further reformation or any other modification, and hence, a need of a well-sophisticated and stronger world system aroused. And the present time of changing circumstances a well-rationalized and restructured organization of such universal system's need is imminent. So, the proposed "The World Union," comprises all countries of the world with equal voting rights, besides it will have all world bodies like UNO, OECD, EU and so on as its members. And then this 'the World Union' will be capable of drafting a befitting plan for peace, progress and prosperity of the world in all possible dimensions. And then between nations the restrictions will be eased out and the countries will be accessible to each other more freely and comfortably.

Peoples' Republic of China is emerging as one of the responsible nations in the global system along with Japan, which was already emerged as highly industrialized nation of the world. So these industrialized nations are drafting a new global social structure, which will be upcoming international system for global economy and global peace. Till recently USA was leading the international systems, and now many other countries are emerging with global stature. The global interdependence and global common good are being promoted by the world organizations like the UNO, UNESCO, the World Trade Organization, International Monetary fund, World Bank and so on. Now once this 'the World Union' comes into its being, it will play pivotal role in resolving all the world conflicts and can establish peace the world over. In fact, in the present scenario, no single country is capable of shouldering higher global responsibilities, nor can deal with global challenges as it was before. That constrained the emergence of a higher global architecture capable of transforming social, economic and political aspects in the world, by developing both nationalism and internationalism as well. Then like that of the fate of a single nation, there will never be any instability to this global system. The spirit of 'the World Union' will be followed by all nations in the world positively. The global equilibrium will be perfectly maintained and that will compensate the power voids left by the earlier dominant nations. Every country wish to have economic growth and equal distribution of wealth the world over and that will become possible through 'the World Union.' Besides consensus of all nations as well can be obtained through the Union within a short span of time, and appropriate decisions can be taken and implemented easily. Transforming the world more interdependent, by maintaining balance of power amongst all nations of the world, all countries will feel happy and comfortable and then the whole world will be peaceful and happy.

As mentioned earlier, the process of uniting the world has already been started and foundations were being laid, starting with the unions of the continents. For example, European Union (EU) was established with the aim of uniting all countries of the Europe, which has 48 countries out which 27 countries became the members of EU and another 8 countries are about to join in it. The norms laid down by EU are applicable to all its member-states and through this it was aspired to unite the whole of the world as well. The well improved norms of this EU may be befitting to the entire world, resulting the emergence of 'the World Union', which will integrate the entire world, and develop the 'universal solidarity and brotherhood.' The fundamental norms will be the global cooperation and collaboration for mutual growth and development. This new 'World Union' will evolve with broadest world vision, to build close and amicable relations between all the nations of the world, forgetting and forgiving all the earlier differences, if at all any, and forge ahead with renewed friendly-tie ups, to help each other, to develop togetherness, and grow together. So this 'World Union' will develop the concept of 'The World is in One,' and will minimize all national identities, besides preserving their sovereignty and independence, and promote the belongingness to the world instead of to a nation or to a continent, which leads men to live happily and without any fears of wars or economic disruptions.

In fact the European Union inspired the regional integration as well in the other continents and as such the other continental unions are also getting evolved namely- North American Union, South American Union, African Union, Union of Australia & New Zealand, Pacific Union, Asian Unions and so on. And so the next sublime transformation for the world will be the formation of "The World Union" comprising of these continental unions. In fact, now no country is daring enough to claim being a continental power or the world power. All countries are aspiring to be a united power together, with a single universal law, following the Universal Code of Conduct and the enforcing power will be the democratic power of all the nations together. Then all nations will concentrate on constructive activities instead of conflicts promoting actions, spear-heading for the creation of the most sophisticated modern world of peace and tranquility. Centuries' struggle for supremacy is coming to an end of late during the present twenty-first century and the centuries in the near future. Any individual nation's ambition of being to be the universal will be subdued after the emergence of this "Universal Union." But initially this 'World Union' may confront some challenges as some countries may oppose with the fearing of losing its sovereignty, but by peaceful negotiations, those countries can be well convinced and with Union's policies of welfare world, and due explanations of its safety and security. In fact, ' the World Union' will be alone capable to shape and model the whole world that can survive without any conflicts, but with constructive vision and goal, mutually beneficial to all nations of the world. All countries in the orbit of 'the World Union' will be well-secured, well-strengthened, and can flourish well with progress and prosperity, having such a huge support from all other nations of the world may be member-states or not. In the 'World Union,' it is highly feasible to correct the erring nation, either by the support of other member-states or by the Union authorities and the help of other non-members (If at all any) can also be taken to resolve any conflicts national or global at ease for the sake of welfare of the whole world. Another important aspect of 'the World Union' will be that all types of "Anti" feelings will automatically subside, namely-the feelings like Anti-American, Anti-European, Anti-African, Anti-Muslim, and so on as " all are one" concept will be promoted and practiced everywhere on this entire globe. It seems that the European Union and Russia are at logger-heads, but the advent of 'the World Union' will diminish all such differences as well. Some of the countries namely-Brazil, Russia, India, China, and such big countries are not within the fold of the European Union and then how will it be possible to achieve its ambition of uniting the world and that constraints the establishment of this 'the World Union.'

In fact, this European Union itself is aspiring a new world order and so the other continental unions. In the evolutionary process, it is not far off for the evolvement of this "the World Union" No other union of the world is aspiring any such power over any other nation, continent or the world, but every nation and every union is thinking in terms of cooperation, collaboration and the development of the world at large collectively, and hence, the emergence of "the World Union" is inevitable. Feeling glorious by the expansionism of their empires was an aspect of the past in the lore, and the fear of wars and invasions had gone on the advent of democratic systems round the globe, besides now is the time for universal solidarity, mutual help and friendship, mutual cooperation and mutual collaboration. Hence, there are no threats, nowhere in the world of today. Everyone everywhere is striving to promote the "spirit of universal solidarity" around the globe.

The prime ambition of the European Union is to transform the world to be a better world and to be a secure world. And so its framework was so designed with such rules and regulations not only to resolve conflicts and for making a country devoid of violence, but also to develop 'universal solidarity and brotherhood' around the globe by all possible means. In fact all countries in the world either war-weary, or war-victim are aspiring for not only peace, amity, and friendship, but also innovation and growth. And hence, the time had ripened for the establishment of such united world system. The sole aim of this European Union is to unite whole of Europe, which was the dream of some earlier emperors of Rome, and some others like Alexander the Great, Genghis Khan, Napoleon Bonaparte, and of late Adolf Hitler, but all were in vain in their attempts. But with the willingness of people on the continent of Europe it had been united without any regional barriers benefitting all of the Europeans and European nations. It was by putting an end to all age-old rivalries between the nations, and uniting them all by merging their interests and building the ties of friendship and solidarity in the true sense. It will be the basis for broader and deeper commitment among people of Europe who suffered long with devastating conflicts and wars for centuries together. And so to preserve and strengthen peace and liberty, and thus, leading to world peace and making it closely interdependent this European Union came into its being. Even though EU has its lofty ideals there is a threat to it by USA as it threatened the EU to undercut it. Hope these conflicts will pacify soon.

As said earlier the continental unions are being formed and numerous international unions are also taking shape. As discussed earlier Brazil, Russia, India, China and South Africa joined hands together and formed an intercontinental union by name as BRICS for mutual cooperation. This forms one-third of the world population. There is another organization by name-The Association of Southeast Asian Nations (ASEAN) consists of ten countries namely- Brunei Darussalam, Cambodia, Indonesia, Lao PDR, Malaysia, Myanmar, Philippines, Singapore Thailand, Vietnam was formed under a Treaty of Amity and Cooperation. The countries of Africa formed as African

Union. Africa has 48 countries and out of them all countries joined in the organization with the main aim of unity and solidarity and to unite all African nations for innovation and growth with mutual cooperation. And so the North American Union, the South American Union and so on, all these follow the exemplary path of European Union. And thus, the power competition will come to an end in the world, when all these continental unions unite and form 'the World Union'. The future world order that is emerging now will be a neoliberal world order-held by this "the World Union." Under its canopy every country should contribute constructively, beneficial for the global community of nations and to the whole of the world at large.

On the emergence of 'the World Union' the challenges it can face and the countries reaction and their contributions can be enlisted as follows:

'The World Union' is a political, universal system evolved out of the centuries of war strife and war-struggle, all the countries decided to unite and work with the following aims and objectives:

1. To promote the world citizenship, amongst those who are well deserved. With this the human relations will be built up the world over and then the universal solidarity and brotherhood will result in, consequently the World Union will become highly strengthened.

2. To promote universal solidarity and brotherhood in all nations of the world.

3. To resolve peacefully with negotiations and treaties, all the disputes and political conflicts between member-states and also between other nations of the world if at all any.

4. To promote cooperation, collaboration, coordination between nations of the world whether members of the union or not. (But invariably all countries of the world will be the members of the union.)

5. To promote global trade, global commerce, global travel and global communications to the best possible way minimizing undue restrictions and practices.

6. To promote research and development globally in all fields with collaboration and cooperation.

7. To promote science, technology and industry; and utilize the advancements globally.

8. To establish international institutions in numerous fields for building up the world well-being.

9. To subdue all regional, national, continental and world conflicts and resolve problems by peaceful dialogues and the Union should play a key role in the deliberations.

10. To shoulder the global safety and security by all possible means.

11. To control arms-race around the globe. Nonproliferation of Nuclear Weapons, manufacturing, distribution and usage are to be dealt with carefully.

12. To deal with all ecological imbalances involving all nations of the world.

13. To promote energy production and deal appropriately the energy conservation and usage.

14. To promote strong ties of amity and friendship between the nations of the world.

15. To build "the World is one "concept and make the world as a harmonious world of peace and tranquility.

16. To develop all nations of the world, supporting weak, disadvantaged and poor countries by all possible means-financial, social, political, and cultural.

17. To avert all world financial crises, by building the best world financial order.

18. To tackle carefully all natural calamities of the world and to support the affected nations in all possible ways.

19. To make significant contribution and aid for the global development and growth.

20. To play pivotal role in almost all global affairs impartially and justifiably.

21. To promote good prospects for prosperous and peaceful world with stability, safety, and security of all countries of the world.

22. To build a new globalized world of interdependence with high economic growth, safe frontiers, and politically stable governments.

Many such challenges can be dealt with by a well-organized international community only, and hence, this 'the World Union' has to be established inevitably. This neo-liberal world order will help the world to grow without un-necessary competition, and without undue economic imbalances. This will be the greatest and unique power in the world and can safe-guard the world of tomorrow. Its prime agenda will be as follows:

1. To achieve global peace, safety and security, besides development and growth

2. To faster friendly relations amongst all nations of the world, minimizing all sorts of disparities namely-economic, social, political and cultural.

3. To promote mutual respect between all nations and honor all treaties and agreements that have been undertaken for the good of the world without fail.

4. To promote peaceful negotiations and/or peaceful settlements of all global conflicts and resolve them amicably.

5. To promote liberal internationalism by global distribution of power and wealth.

6. To stabilize the world democratic system and avoid dominations of all types in the world.

In the recent past the clarion call for a new global architecture of global governance came into its being all over the world and it is Russia that is advocating it highly. Most of the super power countries like Russia, America, Britain, Japan, China, India, and France are playing crucial roles in getting evolved a global system with great interest. Belgium is also wish to have a rule-based international system. The whole world is transforming, briskly, from bi-polar to uni-polar and now to multi-polar and then it will dissolve into the non-polar world or unique-polar world soon. The world if united, then all countries will be its sub-states besides preserving its own independence and sovereignty, but collectively strive for the unity, solidarity, innovation, growth and development. The question of domination does not arise at all and instead of that universal solidarity only reigns supreme. Then all major powers will shape the future global system-the future world to be more peaceful and happy. The United States of America and Russia will jointly contribute strategic balance of power in the world resulting its safety and security. Their collaboration on many global issues is highly welcoming move the world over, and hence, the advancement of the world order is imminent.

With common goals and common agenda distinct countries are associating together and building amity and solidarity and thus, paving the way for the world unity as well. For example, the Organization of Islamic Conference (OIC), which brought fifty-seven Muslim majority countries together for building up amity and solidarity amongst them. Similarly the Shanghai Cooperation Organization (SCO) consisting of the countries namely China, Russia, Kazakhstan, Kyrgyzstan, Tajikistan and Uzbekistan, working together for mutual and international cooperation and collaboration with all friendly tie-ups. Brazil, Russia, India, China and South Africa joined hands together and formed an organization namely BRICS for mutual cooperation and collaboration in various aspects like economic, and political as mentioned earlier. And there is another India, Brazil, and South Africa Dialogue Forum for involving in the world affairs actively. The objective of Organization of Economic Cooperation and Development (OECD) is the same as its name suggests for building welfare world with prospering nations. Another regional organization namely-Asia Pacific Economic Cooperation (APEC) is a group of countries- those are for trans-pacific regional free trade and commerce, also it aims for international leadership. The Black Sea Economic Cooperation (BSEC) is another group of Central Asian countries established for mutual cooperation and collaboration in various economic and political issues, and for maritime collaboration with Russia, and for mutual development and growth. The Association of South-East Asian Nations (ASEAN) consists of the countries namely Brunei Darussalam, Cambodia, Indonesia, Lao PDR, Malaysia, Myanmar, Singapore, Philippines, Thailand, Vietnam, joined hands for mutual help and mutual development in the region. It is well known about the groups of countries namely G_5, G_6, G_7, G_{13}, G_{20}, G_{77}, and so on in which some countries grouped themselves for international cooperation and collaboration in all aspects economic and political.(It has been dealt with about these elsewhere). The foreign policies of most of the countries of the world are promoting and projecting globalization, and global governance, which is equality-based, practicable and multilateral as well. The African Union (AU) is playing a crucial reformist role and assumed leadership in most global issues and for building up multilateral institutions and especially in Non-Aligned Movement the world over. Besides The South Africa Regional Integration Initiative (SARII) is aiming at building better overland lines for communication and transportation to connect all countries in the continent, and thus, bring unity and amity among them. Some international organizations are also working for such global growth and development namely-International Bank for Reconstruction and Development, World Bank, International Monetary Fund, and so on. Needless is to say about the NATO and Warsaw Pact. Organization for Security and Cooperation in Europe is concerned to all European countries for their safety and security and also for their development, which is working along with European Union.

And now some of the countries are aspiring for such international leadership and thus, assuming global responsibility, besides giving priority to their domestic independence and sovereignty, and are vehemently promoting the construction and management of a rule based international system. For example, Brazil is aspiring ardently a global system, South Africa is leading all African countries and supporting for a rule-based international system, Turkey is ambitious to become a global player, which has long standing special relationship with Azerbaijan namely-historical, cultural, religious and ethnic relationships. And even if we consider Iran its political evolution is remarkable, a slow transition from fragmentation to democratic system with international orientation. Its web of multilateral ties is developing significantly. It is also aspiring international integration and wishes to take part in the international community actively in the present advancements in the country and in the world. There are some interesting international relationships that are going on the world scenario. For example, The Forum of China–Africa Cooperation Development came into its being as China showed interest in the development of Africa and it extended its support in scientific, technical and industrial expertise. The Tokyo International Conference on African Development (TICAD) is promoting aid and assistance to Africa showing Japan's involvement in international development. In fact Japan is well committed for global common good. There are more interesting some such international relations namely-US-India Security Ties, US-Japan Alliance, US-Russia Agreement for Peaceful Nuclear Cooperation, US-Russia Cooperation Threat Reduction and so on. The Gulf Cooperation Council (GCC) is an organization, which is establishing stronger ties of friendship and cooperation among the South Arabia and all other countries in the Gulf.   And the collective voices of numerous countries the world over propounding the same since long. Consequently, the conflicting concepts of division, and fractioning and fragmentation due to either with distinct ideologies' or any sort of other differences are all constrained to cease at the behest of such universal system, say, "The World Union." There after there will not be any Western hegemony, or Eastern hegemony; Northern hegemony or Southern hegemony, neither American hegemony nor Russian hegemony, or even the Third World hegemony. To all such aspiring nations to be prominent in the world affairs, 'the World Union' will extend such opportunity by giving the global responsibilities and that promotes high commitment to all the nations equally to work for the welfare of the humanity and of the entire world. Besides having continental organizations for the development like New Partnership of Africa's Development (NEPAD), the world development forum will also come into their being for the overall development of the world, as the whole world unite will be well organized with the unique principle of "Universal Solidarity and brotherhood."

In fact the emerging constraints for such international system, stem from different countries of the world, which besides fulfilling their self-interests, self-identities, self-governance and individual sovereign democracies, those countries unite and propound for a lofty system for establishing a welfare world. So this 'World Union' will keep doors open, welcoming all nations, including the poor and disadvantaged in the present day advancing world , and in whichever way may they be lagging behind-economic, political, social and even cultural. This 'World Union,' which is a global liberal, international system, will extend its helping hand to the wider world, giving high emphasis on human rights and human dignity, and spreading the world wide concept of human values and will build up the needed framework for the world unity, cooperation and collaboration in all possible fields, and thus, mold the new shape for the world and promote the welfare of the humanity predominantly.   Of course UNO and its subsidiary wings like UN Human Rights Commission and UN Human Rights council are working in these directions partially, but their efforts are not up to the mark as the day stands. As the prime motto of this new global system is-The Universal Solidarity, amity and friendship between all nations in world along with mutual cooperation and mutual collaboration amongst them, the peace will be the natural outcome without any further efforts by anyone. It will be the new renaissance the world over.

There are 238 (not all nations enlisted) countries in the world almost all countries are affiliated to some international organizations/institutions with the view of international cooperation and collaboration in different fields and activities establishing that all people in the world are ardently aspiring for the universal solidarity and amity. Greenland, Vatican City, and Taiwan are not UNO members yet. Here we will enlist the memberships of the countries in the concerned organizations to establish how the countries are aspiring instead of any expansionism, or colonization or any type of undue domination aspiring for amity, solidarity, and friendship with mutual cooperation, mutual collaboration and mutual coordination with togetherness. Hence, it further establishes the unity of the world and the emergence of "The World Union" is inevitable, which is the sublime transformation for the world.

United Nations Organization (UNO); Group of countries G_5, (of Europe with entry of Poland it became G_6 of Europe and emerging economies this G_5, of leading economies of group 5 countries of the world **G-5**; The richest economies of the world called the G_6; G_7, G_8, As Russia opted out G_{13} became G_{12}, G_{20}, G_{77} is group of 133 countries joined together for international cooperation; The developing nations group for economic development and for influencing the global issues BRICS came into its being. The European Union has 27 member countries out of 48 European countries. The group of ASEAN consists of ten members for regional collaboration. African Union formed for the unity and amity of African continent having 54 member-states. The Organization of Islamic Conference joined fifty-seven Muslim majority nations joined hands for international amity and development with mutual collaboration and cooperation. There is another Eurasian politico-economic and military organization for international cooperation in these fields with the 6 countries called Shanghai Cooperation Organization (SCO). For the global development nearly 34 counties around the globe formed an Organization namely- Organization of Economic Cooperation and Development (OECD). NATO is alliance of 28 members for international cooperation and development. There was another alliance called Warsaw Pact (WP) for international cooperation and security. The monarchism in the Gulf formed another cooperative forum called Gulf Cooperative Council (GCC) for regional cooperation and development. Only some of the unions/associations have been considered and many may remain. Now we prepare regional wise list of the all countries in the world with their affiliations even though the number of organizations is not exhaustive. South Asian Association of Regional Cooperation (SAARC), League of Arab States (LAS), MINT, Union of South American Nations (UNASUR), North American Union (NAU), Central Asian Union (CAU) is for eternal friendship, Caribbean Community (CARICOM), South African Regional Integration Initiative (SARII) and The Pacific Union (TPU), and so are some associations/unions of some of the countries aspiring international cooperation and solidarity.

Table 8.5

This shows the member-states of UNO and the countries associated with the other countries forming some other organizations for fulfilling certain other aspects for the world welfare like economy, industry, defense, and mutual cooperation and collaboration.

S.No	Country	Continent	Affiliation to Organization
	There are 4 countries	1. North America	
1.	Canada		UNO, G_7, G_8, G_{13}, G_{20}, OECD, NATO, NAU,
2.	Greenland		Not independent country
3	Mexico		UNO, G_{20}, OECD, MINT, NAU,
4.	United States of America		UNO, **G-5**, G_6, G_7, G_{13}, G_{20}, NAU, OECD, NATO,
	There are 21 countries	2. Central America and the Caribbean	
5..	Antigua and Barbuda		UNO, G_{77}, CARICOM,
6.	The Bahamas		UNO, G_{77}, CARICOM,
7.	Barbados		UNO, G_{77}, CARICOM,
8.	Belize		UNO, G_{77}, CARICOM,
9.	Costa Rica		UNO, G_{77},
10.	Cuba		UNO, G_{77},
11.	Dominica		UNO, G_{77}, CARICOM,
12.	Dominican Republic		UNO, G_{77},
13.	El Salvador		UNO, G_{77}, CARICOM,
14.	Grenada		UNO
15.	Guatemala		UNO, G_{77},
16.	Haiti		UNO, G_{77}, CARICOM,
17.	Honduras		UNO G_{77},,
18.	Jamaica		UNO, G_{77}, CARICOM,
19	Mexico		UNO, G_5, G_{13},
20	Montserrat		CARICOM,
21.	Nicaragua		UNO, G_{77},
22.	Panama		UNO, G_{77}, CARICOM,
23.	Saint Kitts and Nevis		UNO, G_{77}, CARICOM,
24.	Saint Lucia		UNO, G_{77}, CARICOM,
25.	Saint Vincent and the Grenadines		UNO, G_{77}, CARICOM,
26.	Trinidad and Tobago		UNO, G_{77}, CARICOM,
	There are 12 countries	3. South America	
27.	Argentina		UNO, G_{20}, G_{77}, UNASUR,
28.	Bolivia		UNO, G_{77}, UNASUR,
29.	Brazil		UNO, G_5, G_{13}, G_{20}, G_{77}, BRICS, UNASUR,

30.	Chile		UNO, G_{77}, OECD, UNASUR,
31.	Colombia		UNO, G_{77}, UNASUR,
32.	Ecuador		UNO, G_{77}, UNASUR,
33.	Guyana		UNO, G_{77}, OIC, UNASUR, CARICOM,
34.	Paraguay		UNO, G_{77}, UNASUR,
35.	Peru		UNO, G_{77}, UNASUR,
36.	Suriname		UNO, G_{77}, OIC, UNASUR, CARICOM,
37.	Uruguay		UNO, G_{77}, UNASUR,
38.	Venezuela		UNO, G_{77}, UNASUR,
	There are 48 countries	**4. Europe**	
39.	*Albania*		*UNO, OIC,NATO,WP,*
40.	*Andorra*		*UNO*
41.	*Armenia*		*UNO,*
42.	*Austria*		*UNO,EU, OECD,*
43.	*Belarus*		*UNO*
44.	*Belgium*		*UNO, EU, OECD, NATO,*
45.	*Bosnia and Herzegovina*		*UNO, G_{77},,*
46.	*Bulgaria*		*UNO, EU, NATO, WP,*
47.	*Croatia*		*UNO, EU, NATO,*
48.	*Cyprus*		*UNO, EU,*
49.	*Czech Republic*		*UNO, EU,OECD, NATO, WP,*
50.	*Denmark*		*UNO, EU, OECD, NATO,*
51.	*Estonia*		*UNO, EU, OECD, NATO,*
52.	*Finland*		*UNO, EU, OECD,*
53.	*France*		*UNO,G_5, G_6, **G-5**, G_6,G_7, G_8, G_{13}, G_{20}, OECD, NATO,*
54.	*Georgia*		*UNO*
55.	*Germany*		*UNO, G_5, G_6, **G-5**, G_6, G_7, G_8, G_{13}, G_{20}, EU, OECD, NATO, WP,*
56.	*Greece*		*UNO, EU, OECD, NATO,*
57.	*Hungary*		*UNO, EU, OECD, NATO, WP,*
58.	*Iceland*		*UNO, OECD, NATO,*
59.	*Ireland*		*UNO, OECD,*
60.	*Italy*		*UNO, G_5, G_6, G_6, G_7, G_8, G_{13}, G_{20}, OECD, NATO,*
61.	*Kosovo*		
62.	*Latvia*		*UNO, EU, NATO,*
63.	*Liechtenstein*		*UNO,*
64.	*Lithuania*		*UNO, EU, NATO,*
65.	*Luxembourg*		*UNO, EU, OECD, NATO,*
66.	*Macedonia*		*UNO,*
67.	*Malta*		*UNO, EU,*
68.	*Moldova*		*UNO,*

69.	Monaco		UNO
70.	Montenegro		UNO
71.	Netherlands		UNO, EU, OECD, NATO,
72.	Norway		UNO, OECD, NATO,
73.	Poland		UNO, G_6, EU, OECD, NATO, WP,
74.	Portugal		UNO, EU, OECD, NATO,
75.	Romania		UNO, EU, NATO, WP,
76.	Russia Federation		UNO, G_8, G_{20}, BRICS, SCO,
77.	San Marino		UNO
78.	Serbia		UNO,
79.	Slovakia		UNO, EU, OECD, NATO, WP,
80.	Slovenia		UNO, EU, OECD, NATO,
81.	Spain		UNO, G_5, G_6, EU, OECD, NATO,
82.	Sweden		UNO, EU, OECD,
83.	Switzerland		UNO, OECD,
84.	Ukraine		UNO
85.	United Kingdom of Great Britain and Northern Ireland		UNO, G_5, G_6, **G-5**, G_6, G_7, G_8, G_{13}, G_{20}, EU, OECD, NATO,
86.	Vatican City		

	There are 27 countries	**5. Asia**	
87.	Bangladesh		UNO, G_{77}, OIC,SAARC,
88.	Bhutan		UNO, G_{77}, SAARC,
89.	Brunei Darussalam		UNO, G_{77},ASEAN, OIC,
90.	Cambodia		UNO, G_{77}, ASEAN,
91.	China		UNO, G_5, G_{13}, G_{20}, G_{77}, BRICS,SCO,
92.	India		UNO, G_5, G_{13},G_{20}, G_{77},BRICS, SAARC,
93.	Indonesia		UNO, G_{20}, G_{77}, ASEAN, OIC, MINT,
94.	Japan		UNO, **G-5**,G_6, G_7,G_8,G_{13}, G_{20}, OECD,
95.	Kazakhstan		UNO, OIC, CAU,
96.	North Korea		UNO, G_{20}, G_{77}, OECD,
97.	South Korea		UNO, G_{20}, OECD,
98.	Kyrgyzstan		UNO, OIC, SCO, CAU,
99.	Laos		UNO, G_{77}, ASEAN,
100.	Malaysia		UNO, G_{77}, ASEAN,OIC,
101.	Maldives		UNO, G_{77}, OIC, SAARC,
102.	Mongolia		UNO, G_{77},
103.	Myanmar		UNO, G_{77}, ASEAN,
104.	Nepal		UNO, G_{77}, SAARC,
105.	Philippines		UNO, G_{77}, ASEAN,

106.	Singapore	*UNO, G₇₇, ASEAN,*
107.	Sri Lanka	*UNO, G₇₇, SAARC,*
108.	Taiwan	*Not independent country*
109.	Tajikistan	*UNO, G₇₇, OIC, SCO, CAU,*
110.	Thailand	*UNO, G₇₇, ASEAN,*
111.	Turkmenistan	*UNO, G₇₇, OIC, CAU,*
112.	Uzbekistan	*UNO, OIC, SCO, CAU,*
113.	Vietnam	*UNO, G₇₇, ASEAN,*
	There are 23 countries	***6. North Africa and Middle East, Greater Arabia.***	
114.	Afghanistan	*UNO,G₇₇, OIC, SAARC,*
115.	Algeria	*UNO, G₇₇, AU, OIC, LAS,*
116.	Azerbaijan	*UNO, OIC,*
117.	Bahrain	*UNO, G₇₇, OIC,GCC, LAS,*
118.	Egypt	*UNO, G₇₇, AU, OIC, LAS,*
119.	Iran	*UNO, G₇₇, OIC,*
120.	Iraq	*UNO, G₇₇, OIC, LAS,*
121.	Israel	*UNO, OECD,*
122.	State of Palestine	*G₇₇, OIC, LAS,*
123.	Jordan	*UNO, G₇₇, OIC, LAS,*
124.	Kuwait	*UNO, G₇₇, OIC, LAS, GCC,*
125.	Lebanon	*UNO, G₇₇, OIC, LAS,*
126.	Libya	*UNO, G₇₇, AU, OIC, LAS,*
127.	Morocco	*UNO, G₇₇, AU, OIC,LAS,*
128.	Oman	*UNO, G₇₇, OIC, GCC, LAS,*
129.	Pakistan	*UNO, G₇₇, OIC, SAARC,*
130.	Qatar	*UNO, G₇₇, OIC, GCC, LAS,*
131.	Saudi Arabia	*UNO, G₂₀, G₇₇, OIC, GCC, LAS,*
132.	Somalia	*UNO, G₇₇, OIC, LAS,*
133.	Syria	*UNO, G₇₇, OIC, LAS,*
134.	Tunisia	*UNO, G₇₇, OIC, LAS,*
135.	Turkey	*UNO, G₂₀, OIC, NATO, MINT,*
136.	United Arab Emirates	*UNO, G₇₇, OIC, GCC, LAS,*
137.	Yemen	*UNO, G₇₇, OIC, LAS,*
	There are 48 countries	***7. Africa and Sub-Sahara***	***Both sovereign democratic republics and kingdoms***
138.	Angola	*UNO, G₇₇,AU,*
139.	Benin	*UNO, G₇₇, AU, OIC,*
140.	Botswana	*UNO, G₇₇, AU,*
141.	Burkina Faso	*UNO, G₇₇, AU, OIC,*
142.	Burundi	*UNO, G₇₇, AU,*

143.	Cameroon		UNO, G_{77}, AU, OIC,
144.	Cape Verde		UNO, G_{77}, AU,
145.	Central African Republic		UNO, G_{77}, AU,
146.	Chad		UNO, G_{77}, AU, OIC,
147.	Comoros		UNO, G_{77}, AU, OIC,
148.	Republic of the Congo		UNO, G_{77}, AU,
149.	Democratic Republic of the Congo		UNO. G_{77}, AU,
150.	Cote d'Ivoire		UNO, G_{77}, AU, OIC,
151.	Djibouti		UNO, G_{77}, AU, OIC,
152.	Equatorial Guinea		UNO, G_{77}, AU,
153.	Eritrea		UNO, G_{77}, AU,
154.	Ethiopia		UNO, G_{77}, AU,
155.	Gabon		UNO, G_{77}, AU, OIC,
156.	The Gambia		UNO, G_{77}, AU, OIC,
157.	Ghana		UNO, G_{77}, AU,
158.	Guinea		UNO, G_{77}, OIC,
159.	Guinea-Bissau		UNO, G_{77}, AU, OIC,
160.	Kenya		UNO, G_{77}, AU,
161.	Lesotho		UNO, G_{77}, AU,
162.	Liberia		UNO, G_{77}, AU,
163.	Madagascar		UNO, G_{77}, AU,
164.	Malawi		UNO, G_{77}, AU,
165.	Mali		UNO, G_{77}, AU, OIC,
166.	Mauritania		UNO, G_{77}, AU, OIC, LAS,
167.	Mauritius		UNO, G_{77}, AU,
168.	Mozambique		UNO, G_{77}, AU, OIC,
169.	Namibia		UNO, G_{77}, AU,
170.	Niger		UNO, G_{77}, AU, OIC,
171.	Nigeria		UNO, G_{77}, AU, OIC, MINT,
172.	Rwanda		UNO, G_{77}, AU,
173.	Sao Tome and Principe		UNO, G_{77},
174	Sahrawi Republic		AU,
175.	Senegal		UNO, G_{77}, AU, OIC,
176.	Seychelles		UNO, G_{77}, AU,
177.	Sierra Leone		UNO, G_{77}, AU, OIC,
178.	South Africa		UNO, G_5, G_{13}, G_{20}, G_{77}, BRICS, AU,
179.	South Sudan		UNO, AU,
180.	Sudan		UNO, G_{77}, AU, OIC,
181.	Swaziland		UNO, G_{77}, AU,
182.	Tanzania		UNO, G_{77}, AU,
183	Togo		UNO, G_{77}, AU, OIC,

184.	Uganda		UNO, G_{77}, AU, OIC,
185.	Zambia		UNO, G_{77}, AU,
186.	Zimbabwe		UNO, G_{77}, AU,
	There are 15 countries	**8. Australia and Oceania**	
187.	Australia		UNO, G_{20}, OECD, TPU
188.	East Timor		UNO, G_{77},
189.	Fiji		UNO, G_{77},
190.	Kiribati		UNO, TPU
191.	Marshall Islands		UNO, G_{77},
192.	Federated States of Micronesia		UNO, G_{77},
193.	Nauru		UNO, G_{77}, TPU
194	New Zealand		UNO, OECD, TPU
195.	Palau		UNO
196.	Papua New Guinea		UNO, G_{77}, TPU
197.	Samoa		UNO, G_{77},
198.	Tonga		UNO, G_{77}, TPU
199.	Tuvalu		UNO, TPU
200.	Vanuatu		UNO, G_{77}, TPU
201.	Solomon Islands		UNO, G_{77}, TPU
**	European Union	**Continental Organization**	G_{20}, OECD

This list in not exhaustive

There are a total of 54 countries or territories that currently are not in the United Nations:

The membership in the UNO is defined by the Charter of UNO (Article 4, Chapter 2). It is open to all peace loving countries, which accept all the obligations in the Charter, after due approval of the General Assembly, and after Security Council's recommendation. In fact all sovereign states can become members of the UNO. There are a total of 54 countries or independent territories that are not members of the UNO at the present. There are four independent Nation-States namely Taiwan, Kosovo, Vatican City, Palestine are not members of UNO.

Dependencies:
American Samoa (US)
Anguilla (GB)
Aruba (NL)
Bermuda (GB)
Bouvet Island (NO)
British Indian Ocean Territory (GB)
British Virgin Islands (GB)
Cayman Islands (GB)
Christmas Island (AU)
Cocos Islands (AU)

Cook Islands (NZ)
Coral Sea Islands Territory (AU)
Falkland Islands (GB)
Faroe Islands (DK)
French Guiana (FR)
French Polynesia (FR)
French Southern Lands (FR)
Gibraltar (GB)
Greenland (DK)
Guadeloupe (FR)
Guam (US)
Guernsey (GB)
Heard and McDonald Islands (AU)
Hong Kong (CN)
Isle of Man (GB)
Jan Mayen (NO)
Jersey (GB)
Macau (CN)
Martinique (FR)
Mayotte (FR)
Montserrat (GB)
Navassa (US)
Netherlands Antilles (NL)
New Caledonia (FR)
Niue (NZ)
Norfolk Island (AU)
Northern Mariana Islands (US)
Pitcairn Island (GB)
Puerto Rico (US)
Reunion (FR)
Saint Helena (GB)
Saint-Pierre and Miquelon (FR)
South Georgia (GB)
Svalbard (NO)
Tokelau (NZ)
Turks and Caicos Islands (GB)
U.S. Minor Pacific Islands (US)
U.S. Virgin Islands (US)
Wallis and Futuna (FR)

Antarctica: Antarctica

Other Areas:

Northern Cyprus - is a self-declared state that is recognized only by Turkey.

Independent Nation States not in the UN:

Taiwan (left the UN when the Republic of China got its seat)

Kosovo

Vatican City -The Holy See holds sovereignty over the state of Vatican City and maintains diplomatic relations with 180 other states. It has been an observer state since 6 April 1964, and gained all the rights of full membership except voting on 1 July 2004.

Palestine - On 29 November 2012 Palestine has been granted the status of non-member observer state. It hasn't (still) been admitted to the UN as a full member.

The responsibility of every nation is for the entire world and
The responsibility of the world is for every nation of the world entire.

IX.The Nations
(For unity and solidarity of all nations and their advancement with amity and friendship)

As in a family every member of it has responsibilities and duties and so in the family of nations every nation has its own responsibilities and duties. The family will be flourishing if every family member is successful and so in the world if every nation triumphs and so the world will be. The family head is responsible for the family and so the leader is highly responsible for the country to be successful. An erroneous family head throws the family into a ditch and so the erroneous leader throws the nation into sea of troubles. His commitment, his policies and his developmental activities alone bring the country to be triumphant. But wonderfully you cannot elect a family head but a leader can be elected if it is a democratic system. In the Human Development Report (HDR) in 1990 the Pakistani Economist Mahabub Ul Haq stated that "People are the real wealth of a nation." If things are taken in this direction every country can become rich. These HDRs are revealing the enlisted nations growth and innovation rather human development, but all nations of the world couldn't be covered.

There are around 238 countries in the world, distributed in the six continents, and some are affluent and well flourishing some are moderately prospering and some other are lagging behind. Now people in the world wish that all countries should grow well and hence, the countries advanced are coming forward to assist the developing and under developing countries to come up, whatever may be the reasons like geographical, economic, social or political. The world as a whole should develop with those efforts by this 'the World Union' as a family of nations as it should be done systematically at a global level. The assistance would be extended in all possible fronts.

Some of the nations in the world already are on the path of progress and prosperity, economically forward, technologically sophisticated, and industrially advanced, besides its geographical and the other economic, social and political advantages, after centuries of hard struggle. Mahabub Ul Haq and the Noble Laureate Amartya Sen had analyzed and ranked the nations' development with Human Development Index (HDI), of almost all nations of the world. This HDI evaluates and quantifies life expectancy, educational levels, and per capita income of the people in a country and rank it as per 2014 report. Out of 7.3 billion people of the world population, around 1.5 billion of people are deprived of proper education, health and standard of life; around one billion are in acute poverty; and around 3.5 billion are lack of social protection; as many as 1.5 billion of workers are in precarious employment, as the report says.

Consider that, about 188 countries in the world that have been ranked on Human Development Index and that report has been published by United Nations Development Program (UNDP). In the report of 2014, the top ranked five countries are Norway, Australia, Switzerland, the Netherlands, and the US; and the last ranked five countries are Niger, Democratic Republic of Congo, Central African Republic, Chad and Sierra Leone. There are medium developed countries also. For the development of the world the countries that are lagging behind should also be well developed by getting matched with advanced countries to less advanced countries, which can be done at global level only.

As per the 2015 HDI the rankings in four categories of the countries are as follows:

1. Very High Human Development

[1.Norway, 2. Australia, 3. Switzerland, 4. Denmark, 5. Netherlands, 6. Germany, 6. Ireland, 8. United States, 9. Canada. 9. New Zeeland, 11. Singapore, 12. Hong Kong 13. Liechtenstein, 14. Sweden, 14. United Kingdom, 16. Iceland, 17. Republic of Korea, 18. Israel, 19. Luxembourg 20. Japan, 21. Belgium, 22. France, 23. Austria, 24. Finland, 25. Slovenia, 26. Spain, 27. Italy, 28. Czech Republic, 29.Greece, 30. Estonia, 31. Brunei Darussalam, 32. Cyprus, 32.Qatar, 34. Andorra, 35. Slovakia, 36. Poland, 37. Lithuania, 37. Malta, 39.South Arabia, 40. Argentina, 41. United Arab Emirates, 42. Chile, 43. Portugal, 44. Hungary, 45. Bahrain, 46.Latvia 47. Croatia, 48. Kuwait, 49. Montenegro,]

2. High Human Development

[50. Belarus, 50. Russian Federation, 52. Omen, 52. Romania, 52. Libya, 55. Bahamas, 56. Kazakhstan, 57. Barbados, 58. Antigua and Barbuda, 59. Bulgaria, 60. Palau, 60. Panama, 62. Malaysia, 63. Mauritius, 64. Seychelles, 64. Trinidad and Tobago, 66. Serbia, 67. Cuba, 67. Lebanon, 69. Costa Rica, 69. Iran, 71. Venezuela (Bolivarian Republic), 72. Turkey, 73. Sri Lanka, 74. Mexico, 75. Brazil, 76. Georgia, 77. Saint Kitts and Nevis, 78. Azerbaijan, 79. Grenada, 80. Jordan, 81. Macedonia, 81. Ukraine, 83. Algeria, 84. Peru, 85. Albania, 85, Armenia, 85. Bosnia and Herzegovina 88. Ecuador, 89. Saint Lucia, 90. China, 90. Fiji, 90. Mongolia, 93. Thailand, 94. Dominica, 94. Libya, 96. Tunisia, . 97. Columbia, 97. Saint Vincent and the Grenadines, 99. Jamaica, 100. Tonga, 101. Belize, 101. Dominican Republic, 103. Suriname, 104. Maldives, 105. Samoa,]

3. Medium Human Development

[106. Botswana, 107. Maldova, 108. Egypt, 109. Turkmenistan, 110. Gabon, 110. Indonesia, 112. Paraguay, 113. Palestine, 114. Uzbekistan, 115. Philippines, 116. El Salvador, 116. South Africa, 116. Vietnam, 119. Bolivia, 120. Kyrgyzstan, 121. Iraq, 122. Carbo Verde, 123. Micronesia, 124. Guyana, 125. Nicaragua, 126. Morocco, 126. Namibia, 128. Guatemala, 129. Tajikistan, 130. India, 131. Honduras, 132. Bhutan, 133. Timor Leste, 134. Syria, 134. Venuatu, 136. Republic of Cango, 137. Kiribati, 138. Equatorial Guinea, 139. Zambia, 140. Ghana, 141. Laos, 142. Bangladesh, 143. Cambodia, 143. Soatome Principe,]

4. Low Human Development

[145. Kenya, 145. Nepal, 147. Pakistan, 148. Myanmar, 149. Angola, 150 Swaziland, 151. Tanzania, 152. Nigeria, 153. Cameroon, 154. Madagascar, 155. Zimbabwe, 156. Muaritania, 156. Solomon Islands, 158. Papua New Guinea, 159 Comoros, 160. Yemen, 161. Lesotho, 162. Togo, 163. Haiti, 163 Rwanda, 163. Uganda, 166. Benin, 167. Sudan, 168.Djibouti, 169. South Sudan, 170. Senegal, 171. Afghanistan, 172. Ivory Coast, 173. Malawi, 174. Ethiopia, 175. Zambia, 176. Democratic Republic of Congo, 177. Liberia, 178. Guinea Bissau, 179. Mali, 180. Mozambique, 181. Syria Leone, 182. Guinea, 183. Burkina Faso, 184. Burundi, 185. Chad, 186. Eretria, 187. Central African Republic, 188. Niger.]

Unluckily some of the countries are not within the purview of the UNDP; they are Greenland, Montserrat, Kosovo, Monaco, Saint Marino, Vatican City, North Korea, Taiwan, Somalia, Saharawi Republic, Tanzania, Marshall Islands, Nauru, Tuvalu, and Hong Kong.

These modern nations became so advanced in science and technology, developed industrially and Consequently, turned out sophisticated and highly opulent. They are benevolently coming forward to extend their helping hand economically to the poorer nations.

There are some more countries to be ranked and enlisted in this HDR, which are not available as the day stands. For the world development those countries should also be considered and their development also matters. If some pairing is made, by considering 188 countries say, then there will be around ninety four pairings and after a few years these ninety four pairings will be grouped again into forty seven pairs of pairs. And in each such pair of pairs there will be four countries, two advanced and two other less advanced in the group and work together with unity they develop in all dimensions. All other countries will also be considered and grouped. For example the twinning may be as follows: The number indicates their ranking in the 2015 HDI listing.

(1.Norway, 96. Tunisia); (2. Australia, 97. Columbia); (3. Switzerland, 97. Saint Vincent and the Grenadines); (4. Denmark, 99. Jamaica); (5. Netherlands, 100. Tonga,); (6. Germany, 101. Belize); (6. Ireland, 101. Dominican Republic); (8. United States, 103. Suriname,); (9. Canada, 104. Maldives); (9. New Zeeland,105. Samoa); (11. Singapore, 106. Botswana); (12. Hong Kong,107. Maldova); (13. Liechtenstein,108. Egypt); (14. Sweden,109. Turkmenistan); (14. United Kingdom,110. Gabon); (16. Iceland,110. Indonesia); (17. Republic of Korea, 112. Paraguay); (18. Israel,113. Palestine,); (19. Luxembourg, 114. Uzbekistan); (20. Japan, 115. Philippines); (21. Belgium,116. El Salvador,); (22. France, 116. South Africa); (23. Austria,116. Vietnam); (24. Finland,119. Bolivia); (25. Slovenia,120. Kyrgyzstan); (26. Spain,121, Iraq); (27. Italy, 122. Carbo Verde); (28. Czech Republic, 123Micronesia); (29.Greece, 124. Guyana); (30. Estonia, 125. Nicaragua); (31. Brunei Darussalam, 126. Morocco); (32. Cyprus, 126. Namibia); (32.Qater, 128. Guatemala,); (34. Andorra,129. Tajikistan); (35. Slovakia,130. India); (36. Poland,131. Honduras,); (37. Lithuania,132. Bhutan); (37. Malta133. Timor Leste); (39.South Arabia,134. Syria); (40. Argentina,134. Venuatu) ; (41. United Arab Emirates, 136. Republic of Cango); (42. Chile, 137. Kiribati); (43. Portugal, 138. Equatorial Guinea); (44. Hungary,139. Zambia); (45. Bahrain 140. Ghana); (46.Latvia, 141. Laos); (47. Croatia,142. Bangladesh); (48. Kuwait, 143. Cambodia); (49. Montenegro, 143. Soatome Principe);

(50. Belarus,145. Kenya); (50. Russian Federation, 145. Nepal); (52. Omen, 147. Pakistan); (52. Romania, 148. Myanmar); (52. Libya,149. Angola); (55. Bahamas,150 Swaziland,); (56. Kazakhstan,151. Tanzania); (57. Barbados,152. Nigeria); (58. Antigua and Barbuda, 153. Cameroon); (59. Bulgaria, 154. Madagascar); (60. Palau, 155. Zimbabwe); (60. Panama, 156. Muaritania) (62. Malaysia, 156. Solomon Islands) (63. Mauritius, 158. Papua New Guinea); (64. Seychelles, 159 Comoros); (64. Trinidad and Tobago,160. Yemen); (66. Serbia, 161. Lesotho); (67. Cuba, 162. Togo); (67. Lebanon, 163. Haiti); (69. Costa Rica, 163 Rwanda,); (69. Iran, 163. Uganda); (71. Venezuela

(Bolivarian Republic), 166. Benin); (72. Turkey, 167. Sudan); (73. Sri Lanka, 168.Djibouti); (74. Mexico, 169. South Sudan); (75. Brazil, 170. Senegal); (76. Georgia, 171. Afghanistan); (77. Saint Kitts and Nevis, 172. Ivory Coast); (78. Azerbaijan, 173. Malawi); (79. Grenada, 174. Ethiopia); (80. Jordan, 175. Zambia); (81. Macedonia, 176. Democratic Republic of Congo); (81. Ukraine, 177. Liberia); (83. Algeria, 178. Guinea Bissau); (84. Peru, 179. Mali); (85. Albania, 180. Mozambique); (85, Armenia,181. Syria Leone); (85. Bosnia and Herzegovina, 182. Guinea); (88. Ecuador, 183. Burkina Faso); (89. Saint Lucia, 184. Burundi); (90. China, 185. Chad);(90. Fiji, 186. Eretria); (90. Mongolia, 187. Central African Republic); (93. Thailand, 188. Niger); (94. Dominica, 94. Libya).

This twinning may be further modified in so many different and convenient ways at the will of the concerned countries. There should be global efforts in the transfer of technical know-how and promoting knowledge and social and political awareness as well. Education and religion are the prime factors that influence advancement besides other geological and physical factors like environmental and climatic. By such matching these can be well addressed by those developing countries. As mentioned earlier some such efforts are going on, for example Japan's endeavors to help African countries. Individual country's efforts cease now and global efforts will commence more systematically.

It is well-known that, ignorance and corruption, which are the two evil factors that hamper the growth of any country. A leader who is corrupted leads the country to a pathetic plight by all possible means. That corruption cripples any nation, and ultimately people suffer. So a perfect person should alone be elected. Therefore, the electorates should be well knowledgeable and non-corruptive. Hence proper education should be imparted in the country from elementary level to university level and bring the masses to that knowledgeable-level, such that they can understand the election process and about the leaders to be elected well, by having such social awareness.
And thus, when best leaders come to the helm, the countries definitely will flourish and consequently the world will be. Besides the people will live happily qand peacefully all over the globe.

Out of these 188 countries there were divided into four groups namely very high, high, medium and low human development. The 2015 report says that the human development is impressive when compared to the earlier reports in terms of life expectancy, elementary and school education, per capita income, and sanitation and clean drinking water availability. Adding to that transportation and telecommunication drastically improved the world over that improved the standard of life of the people also.

Some countries suffered with political conflicts and in civil disturbances, some other suffered with the vagaries of nature, making people to bear all along with loss of their properties besides hindering their work and employment. Consequently, the human potentiality gone waste, and remained un-utilized. If the human potential is completely taped, and if every individual works to his capacities to the brim, the world development will be imminent. The human development, national development and world development are all interlinked. The able workers both skilled and unskilled have to be considered for this purpose. But gender discrimination became a hurdle for such growth. This should be properly addressed by every nation for its growth and innovation.

Technical advancements and globalization contributed much for the national development and as well the world development. In any country unemployment rate should be zero, as it will be a great loss to the nation if one person's work is lost, for any reason, as work not provided, not available, the person is unwilling or lethargic. So the national government should take meticulous care in utilizing the human potential, taking justifiable considerations about their rights and the feasibility, for the country.

We need a global comprehensive plan for such steps to be taken. In some sectors like energy and industry, science and technology, agriculture and animal welfare, medicine and hygiene only worldwide united efforts are highly beneficial. Besides trade, commerce and business will be highly profitable when it is of worldwide united effort. In this worldwide united activity every country will be involved and every country will be developed automatically.

The teaching methodologies, the educational concepts with the worldwide knowledge should be imparted, besides, best ideas of life and living. Hence teachers at all levels should be well trained with the latest concepts who will impart better knowledge to the masses in the best possible way.

Universal Health Care may be adapted worldwide, nullifying exploitation in the field. In UK medical aid is free. For the advancement of human development, which will sustain the world with progress and prosperity, the national governments should adapt the best policies with commitment. Transfer of medical technology and training of medical personal, at all levels from physicians, surgeons, midwifes to nurses worldwide will help enhance the human welfare and consequently, the national development or even the world development In any country the human power and especially the youth power are highly important, as they contribute to the development. So no man-hour to be wasted and for that the national plans should be well-tuned. For example, the employment and work policies of the government should be so perfect with equal wages for men and women, the work environment should be clean and hygienic, and the employer and employees relations should be so congenial. For achieving this too, the national policies should be too good, without hampering the rights of the employees, and should be considerate to their problems.

The Global Forum on Migration and Development with more than 150 countries of the world is to be further extended to almost all countries of the world, and that is to be further strengthened to facilitate immigrants and the workforce that increases opportunities and resulting in the human development and national as well. For that further the concerned nations should look after the immigrants' well-being and ensure their rights and responsibilities with meticulous care. In this rapidly changing world for the sake of human progress the concerned national governments should make structural changes in the society such that the work turns out to be more creative and beneficial.

All the countries should develop in all possible dimensions by putting ahead with certain goals for growth and prosperity utilizing the complete human potential, to develop creativity, innovation and growth without any gender disparity, with global concern and commitment.

It is Amartya Sen, who opened our eyes with his illuminating concept of human welfare and human development and consequently the world development with mutual cooperation and mutual coordination. The ranking of almost all countries in the world as given above helps each country to assess itself and make efforts to improve its stature for getting international development.

For achieving these results we absolutely need an international body, which should be authoritative, but not just advisory as UNO. That can enforce the national governments to look after the human well-being; resulting in the societies' well-being and in succession the national and world well-being takes place.

Even though the social progress is going on since time immemorial, now as the whole world is making rapid strides in all dimensions, no one country can shoulder the development of the world by considering each and every country, but all advanced countries should take such a joint responsibility.

If the national government knows the best use of human energy of the country, and its most productive and the most creative capacities, for the common good of all people in the country and if all nations work appropriately in this direction then it will led to the greatest common good of the world itself. Each country should be a role model in all possible fronts, for the rest of the countries with the spirit of perfect liberty amongst its citizens and with the spirit of pure and perfect competition amidst the countries in the world, then the whole world will flourish, gloriously with all peace and prosperity. Every individual should behave befittingly and work for the general good of the society, in order for their country to prosper. The country which uses its human energy to the fullest extent will be alone the richest.

The human capital of the nations should also be well utilized by the universal government, its ingenuity, its intelligence, its creativity and its productivity for the whole world, to bring up all countries and their societies in the world.

In fact some of the countries couldn't grow well, without any external assistance and aid, because of so many reasons like political aspects of the nation, climatic and geographical conditions. Some nations are growing fast and becoming rich and some other nations are becoming poor because of the land, its fertility; its natural resources, extreme weather conditions, and un-utilized human potential energies, and any one country like United States of America, or Russian Federation, or UK cannot shoulder the responsibilities of all some such countries in the world. It should be done on global scale only. Hence a well organized universal set up is certainly needed.

The productive power of the man must be best utilized by all nations in the world, if the countries have civilized societies, but in the case of countries with uncivilized, savaged, and barbaric societies, those countries should be educated and trained to become well-sophisticated to serve the society well. These societies usually covered with the veil of ignorance and superstition, and by proper education that should be taken off. Then those countries will become powerful and cultured. The power of intelligentsia is an essential aspect of any nation. This is a big task ahead on this universal body to harp on.

As building up the development process the world over is such a herculean task, beyond the scope of any country, the division of labor would be the best policy. For this there should be a universal revolution to transform the whole world. The power of a nation and the power of the world dependent on the immeasurable power of human intelligence, if utilized well, then the wealth of the world will increase infinite folded.

Besides, for the progress of any nation, trade, commerce and industry, both domestic and global, play pivotal role. So it should be keenly noted that global trade and business should be inevitably developed by building such a global set up. But there should be clean, healthy and perfect competition with mutual understanding.

In those earliest, rudest and hardest times of the society, the humanity totally lived on hunting and fishing alone, exposed to the extreme and severe climatic conditions, and thus, suffered unbearably all their lives. The time rolled on with consistent development and the culture advanced and the life styles and living standards simultaneously enhanced. And the countries transformed into well civilized countries. Then emerged the kings and kingdoms; emperors and empires, and consequently wars. The whole world and all its continents were under the grip of strife and struggle, but besides these the world made rapid strides of development in all fronts, consistently improving. And all countries were gravitating between riches and poverty, as some countries developed their productive power to the highest extent and some others are lagging behind uncultured, poverty-stricken. In fact the corruptive and selfish leaders ruined their own countries with all their wrong practices and policies. Hence those countries without any progress remained uncivilized and undeveloped and under developed.

In the developed countries, the national wealth tremendously increased and became most elegant, sophisticated countries of the world, but in the poorer countries, the people faced terrific hardships, and in these countries it was a declining state of affairs in all dimensions, poverty, hunger and disease reigned supreme.

But at the beginning of this present century it was an ingenious idea of '*twinning*' a well civilized country to a less civilized country for the mutual development, so that all countries will develop and hence, the whole world will advance with great rapidity.

In fact the prosperity of any country depends on many a factor, including its human power utilization, for example, China has been long, one of the richest countries of the world as it is one of the highly fertile, most cultured, remarkably industrious and having well utilized human potential, besides most populous in the world. So we can say that the wealth of that country is very high. And the acquisition of riches year by year further by that country is significant and there will be utmost prosperity for that country. And so is Japan.

Some of the countries in Northern America and in Europe are progressing so rapidly such that the wealth of those nations became directly proportional to the increase of population of those countries, with the human potential power harnessed perfectly well, resulting great prosperity. And when the states are with such progress and prosperity, the people will also be very happy and cheerful, and welcome heartily some of the people of other states as well, but if the states are static, or are declining, what so ever may be the reason, political, social, economic, the people will be in melancholy, dull and docile hampering the tranquility of the state, which turns out to be a great impediment for the world growth and development. So the 'Twinning' of the countries through this 'the World Union' will help excellently.

In the past, the prosperity or decline of any empire small or great, resulted in, the rise and fall of the constituent countries, consequently the progress and prosperity of those countries as well. That is the increase and decrease of the state of the wealth of the society, affecting every individual well-being and the country's well-being too. Fortunately, the monarchism faded away and almost all countries assumed democratic republic governments, getting full freedom and liberty and that paved the way for progress and prosperity. And the countries either of the same continent or of different continents developed interdependence, consequently amity and unity became a certainty between nations the world over.

Some of the industrious nations are advancing so rapidly by acquiring riches as the industrious individuals of the country and hence, the country too is growing fast. But in some countries the ruinous administrators at the helm, with his ill-planning and hazardous policies wreck the nation itself causing hazardous problems to its citizens. For example, if we consider the remote past, as said earlier, hunting and fishing were the prime avocations in that rude and rough state of the society, and what they earned was insufficient for their livelihood. In the changing circumstances, in the advanced state of the society many new avocations came forth, making individuals rich and the country turned out to be rich, rising to the commanding positions in the world.

The prosperity and advancement of any country depends on the productive labor and the work force of the people of the country. Hence the people are the real wealth of any nation. Of course land and the other natural resources are the durable part of the wealth of the nation. For an extensive country the land is highly resilient. And the real wealth of the society is its intelligentsia. Besides the real capital of the country is totally based on whether the inhabitants of it are industrious or idle. Thus, the principal cause of the rapid progress of any country towards wealth and greatness is in investing their whole capitals, like individual work potential, hither to employ in agriculture. And then the country will progress well, resulting in human prosperity. This has been well established by China, with its wonderful accounts of wealth and accumulation. That wealth of the country leads to economic stability, and economic power, and that further leads to political power as well and then the country will emerge powerful in all aspects. And thus, the countries, which practiced such principles, become the richest countries in the world in which the capitals of the individuals invested for the whole of the society, the whole of the country and whole of the world.

Hence the progress of opulence of any country solely depends on the men inhabited in the country. And besides the human potential, every just government of the country should have such policies aiming at the prosperity of the country and that means the well-being of every citizen of the country. When the agriculture is well developed in the country then that contributes the development of the industries- that further leads to well-utilization of man power of it.

There are two types of countries in the world namely advantageous and disadvantageous. The advantageous countries are trivially wealthier than the disadvantageous. Then the challenge lies in enriching the disadvantageous countries as well, with the scientific and technological advancements. With the well advanced technical knowhow, people will develop expertise to utilize fully-well that whatever is available in those disadvantageous countries, for the human use, and such utility increases, industries will automatically develop in its consequence.

The first duty of any sovereign state is to protect the society from unjust, oppression, violence and invasions of the other independent societies that can be performed by means of military force only. From the first ages of the society the war was an inevitable phenomenon that occurred all over the world in the last two millennia. The degree of perfection that is increasing in the human activity the social and political evolution also took place, and hence, the advancement of society and the state resulted in. Consequently, people around the globe aspired for peace profound. More civilized the country become; the wisdom of the country molded it for progress and prosperity. In fact the barbarous nations required military force, weaponry and forts but the civilized nations required goodwill ambassadors who are capable of enriching both the society and the state leading to the progress of the opulence of the country.

And thus, after the advent of this 'The World Union', with the global efforts of this Union, the whole world and all the countries of the world will be on the path of peace, progress and prosperity. And hence the whole world will definitely develop in all fronts.

X. The World Trade, Business and Commerce
(For global trade and the globalization with mutual cooperation of all nations)

For the development of the nations, international trade will play pivotal role, because the business needs are such in the world. And because raw materials, manufacturers, consumers may be available in different countries and the agricultural produce may be abundant in one country and the consumption may be in a different country. In the advanced state of a country the technical knowhow may be exceedingly higher than in the less advanced countries. And hence, to curtail such disparities international trade is to be developed to a much higher level. The 'Twinning" will help- a lot in this aspect. The other aspect is the 'Globalization.' The World Trade Organization is to be further strengthened and to be extended to the entire world involving all the countries, besides associating with the World Union, as this development can be done at a global level.

For achieving perfect goal of world unity, the universal currency may be brought in, which will be the commanding currency of the world and the world economy and each country will fix up the exchange rates. The currency may be in coins and notes,which will be very high quality and the coins preferably of gold and silver.

XI. The Charter of the World Union
(The universal constitution with universal code of conduct)

The Preamble states that

> We, the inhabitants of the globe and the citizens of this world agreed and united firmly to resolve

- For progress and prosperity, for the well-being of all humans on the globe, to live with peace and tranquility

- For achieving the universal solidarity and brotherhood, to promote mutual cooperation and mutual coordination among all people in the world and amidst all nations of the world

- For the development of every human being and consequently every nation

- Universal progress and prosperity, universal advancement, universal safety and security

- That being the ultimate destiny of the humankind,

- To preserve and further built the unity of the whole humanity, for their advancement and opulence in all dimensions and directions

- For making the democratic governance in all nations, and at all levels in the nation

- And keeping the independence and sovereignty of each and every nation intact,

- As the world faced numerous calamities and catastrophes, some natural and some other man-made

- As the whole of mankind experienced immeasurable sorrow and suffering for centuries together

- As the whole world has to develop by avoiding any further such misery and melancholy

- And to believe the human importance and intelligence and, to develop equality and equanimity amongst all men in the world and amidst all nations in the world.

- to find solutions to all problems and conflicts in the world more amicably and justifiably by sheer negotiations and treaties and by mutual consultations and discussions

- To advance better social relations with high standard of life and living, with all over prevailing justice.

- To maintain tolerance of distinct ideologies and develop mutual understanding and thus, to maintain peace and tranquility the world over,

- To mold all people of the world to live with togetherness, culture and friendship

- To pledge not to wage war by any country on any other, instead develop more international organizations for building up economic, social, political stability the world over.

- To develop the world scientifically, technologically and industrially for the welfare of the whole world.

- And every individual and every nation to follow the universal code of conduct,

- And protect the freedom and liberty of every person on the planet,

- To elect one such government on the name of 'The World Union'

- Which is defined as- *of the nations, by the nations and for the nations*

- To establish this charter and to obey it as it is the law of this "The World Union."

- **And to achieve these goals**

We, the heads/representatives of all countries of the world met in Washington DC, and resolved to join hands for- to work together united, and endorse a high statured and powerful world body by name "The World Union" and empower it to do all the things needed to accomplish these above goals.

The Charter

- The charter of the "The World Union" is the fundamental agreement of the Union, comprising of all the nations of the world willing for such unity of the world, believing and willing to work for *Universal Solidarity and brotherhood with Mutual Cooperation and Co-ordination, amongst all people and amidst all nations of the world.* It was signed in Washington DC by all willing member states on February 10, 2016 in the first instant and will be signed by all nations in the world as and when they join and support the Union.

Chapter. 1: The need of the World Union

Articles

1. This constitution is covenanted and pledged for imparting universal justice to all people and all nations in the world, as a matter of right
2. The world Union has well defined jurisdiction, as bestowed by this charter
3. The charter can be enforced on all its member-states by the Union
4. Both the rights of man and the rights of the nations propounded here, and every person and every nation can enjoy besides all the privileges of the constitution, but should shoulder the responsibilities of the World Union as well.
5. The universal code of conduct is to be followed by all people and all nations strictly and it is also mandatory and enforceable.
6. In view of safety and security and peace, progress and prosperity, the amendments made by the TWU is binding on all nations and all people in the world
7. All disputes and conflicts are being solved peacefully by the TWU, and it is the final decision that is binding and to be strictly adhered to.
8. Maintaining peace and tranquility, the TWU will keep on an eye on the development of all countries, with mutual collaboration, mutual cooperation and mutual coordination and all nations should extend its help and support by all means without fail

9. War and Violence are hindrances for the growth and prosperity and hence strictly prohibited by the TWU, and all nations should invariably support the cause for such prohibition and cooperate with the TWU. Its decision is final.

10. From time to time special offices for temporary or permanent need maybe installed to fulfill certain tasks like arbitration, negotiation and so on, and the TWU in empowered for the same.

11. The TWU will plan the budget and levy the costs on the member-states, who have to pay the dues invariably.

12. The TWU's Development Bank and all fiscal policies are within the purview of the TWU

13. The TWU policies regarding Trade, business and industry, are binding on all business and industrial organizations of all member-states

14. The laws concerning emigration and immigration are to be strictly adhered to by all nations. The authority of issuance of The Universal Citizenship Passport for the deserving lies with TWU

15. To serve the society, country, continent and the world to the best of one's ability

16. To follow the principles for peace, progress and prosperity.

17. To preserve and protect unity and solidarity of all nations of the world.

18. ***To realize that The World Union" is- by the nations, of the nations, for the nations***

19. In this connection every person and every nation have the bounden commitment for the society and for the world, for the universal code of conduct as propounded by the charter of the World Union, which is enforceable at all times

20. Have right to live comfortably and independently beyond poverty with pride and prestige

21. Have right to safety and security without facing any exploitation

22. Have the right for full freedom and liberty

23. Have the right to be in democratic rule and to follow the principles of democracy at all levels

24. Have the right to follow one's own culture, religion and faith without any external influences

25. The rights of the people or nations will be protected by the GWC and Council of Law and Justice and the Court of Justice

26. To maintain peace and justice in all nations of the world by resolving all problems, both domestic and amidst nations in the world, with amicable solutions, agreeable for the both parties with the prime principle of justice and with adjustment, accord and agreement.

27. To maintain congenial and serene social environment, by building up religious tolerance, to minimize ideological differences, and to build friendly world of nations and world of friendly citizens.

28. All the natural resources can be utilized by all individuals, all nations and the world at free will within the granted power by law of the nature and this constitution, without affecting the general interests of the society, nation or the world.

29. To establish such international institutions under the canopy of the World Union, for shouldering different aspects of the world namely economic, political, social, philanthropic, and humanitarian.

30. To promote universal solidarity and brotherhood without any discrimination of race, region; religion, caste, creed and country; gender, economic status, and language. It is the sole aim of preserving the freedom and liberty of every individual on the face of the earth and every nation in the world.

31. To build a harmonious world of peace and tranquility without any complexes of superiority and inferiority; domination and subjugation, but with affable and friendly relations between nations and between the people.

32. The members of the Union, in order to accomplish the above goals, should work with meticulous care and consideration when any conflict arose, preserving one's own sovereignty and allowing others as well, without going for confrontation by any means.

33. This Charter of the Union awards certain rights and benefits besides duties and obligations for all its member states, for which all are bound inevitably without exemptions and make their people and the nations to follow the *universal code of conduct* defined by the Union.

34. All differences and disputes between nations should be invariably resolved by justifiable and peaceful means on the principles of safety and security, without endangering the peaceful and friendly coexistence of the nations.

35. It is mandatory to all member-states of the Union to support strongly in all its activities and programs for the welfare of the world. Even if any difference arose between the Union and any nation, it should be amicably settled with the sole aim of preserving congenial and friendly relations.

36. Mandatorily, all countries of the world should be the members of the Union, and should follow the precepts of the Union in Toto to preserve peace, progress and prosperity of all nations of the world.

37. It is the country's obligation to bring even the domestic problems, to the notice of the World Union or the Continental Union and get it resolved amicably to preserve safety and security of the country and to get it channelized towards progress and prosperity.

Chapter 2. The Membership in the Union

38. It is mandatory that all nations numbering nearly 238 be the members of the Union, irrespective of their stature, in any aspects like area (small or big), economic status and population. And all nations will be treated equally without any discrimination.

Chapter 3. The Union and its subsidiary bodies.

39. The main body is called "The World Union" that consists of six continental unions namely-
The North American Continental Union,
The South American Continental Union,
The African Continental Union,
The European Continental Union (the reformed union of the European Union)

The Asian Continental Union.

The Australian and New Zeeland Continental Union with all its Pacific Islands

The Polar Regions namely the North Polar Region and South Polar Region are two totally independent states but under the purview of the World Union.

The Head Quarters of the Union has the following main offices namely-

All member-states of The World Union will be called the General World Council.

So the World Union consists of the following councils for the needed Union's activities namely-

The World Union's General Council or

The General World Council (GWC) (with Supreme administrative powers of the Union)

The Union's Secretariat (US)

The Union's Council for Peace, Security and Safety (CPSS)

The Union's Council for Defense Strategies (CDS)

The Union's Council for Progress and Prosperity (CPP)

The Union's Council for Philanthropic and Humanitarian Activities (CPHA)

The Union's Council for Scientific, Technological and Industrial Development (CSTID)

The Union's Council for Research and Development (CRD)

The Union's Council for Trade, Commerce and Business (CTCB)

The Union's Council for Economic, Social and Political Affairs (CESPA)

The Union's Council for Human Resource Development (CHRD)

The Union's Council for Law and Justice (CLJ)

The Union's Court of Justice (CJ)

The Union's Council for Fine Arts and Culture (CFAC)

The Union's United World Educational Organization (UWEO)

The Union's Council for Agriculture, Farming and Animal Welfare (CAFAW)

The Union's Council of Human Health and Medical Related Issues (CHHMRI)

40. Its subsidiary offices will be in the respective Continental Union Offices, such that all countries will be committed and involved in the world development process.

41. Their formation, their functions will be further dealt with in detail and its powers will also be well defined. All these Councils further empowered to built their own organizational structures keeping an eye over the world welfare and thus, involving all the countries of the world. All the unions and councils should work with the sole principle of

"The World Union" is- by the nations, of the nations, and for the nations
"Every nation's responsibility is for the entire world and the world's responsibility is for every nation of the world entire."
Thus "the World Union" will be the savior, servant and master of supreme stature of the entire world.

42. Finally, the provision for 'the World Citizens' will be defined by the men who will be well concerned for the welfare society of the world, who will endeavor for "*Universal Solidarity and brotherhood with Mutual Cooperation and Mutual Co-ordination.*", by activity or by profession, and are moving round the globe in propagation and practice of this motto.

3.a. The World Union

43. The World Union is bestowed with certain powers, and member-states should invariably oblige them

44. The World Union is - by the nations, of the nations, for the nations

45. The World Union is having its legislature as follows:
    The Parliament
    The Director General
    The Councils
    Some special offices needed
    The General World Council and the Secretary General
    The Union's Court of Justice
    The Union's Council of Law and Justice
    All continental unions and regional unions are just replica of the World Union only

Chapter 4. Formation, Functions, Powers, Voting and Principles and procedures of the General World Council (GWC).

This is the prime body of 'the World Union,' followed by all other councils,

46. The General World Council will have 238 members (Depending the number of countries) who are the heads of the states who came to that position on democratic means, have the voting right. Each such member has another representative, to look after the commitments, in the case of the absence of the member, and can also cast his vote on his/her behalf as proxy vote. In certain elections where peoples' referendum is needed, the strength of the vote depends on the population of the country counting 100k as one unit, and part thereof if it is more than 50k. In case of the countries with less population a group of countries may join together to qualify, if the strength of population is 100k one unit will be granted to them. If less than 50k that may be combined with some other country.

47. The member will vote in some occasions individually and some other occasions with the strength of the vote where and when peoples' referendum is needed.

48. The GWC will meet every year in January and work for 15 days, without any break, to discuss the development activities of the world.

49. The GWC will have six electoral colleges pertaining to, to the six continents namely North America, South America, Europe, Africa, Asia, and Australia & New Zeeland.

50. The language of the TWU will be English as the main language and other languages will have due importance and will be made use of as per the occasion.

51. From the six continental heads, one will be elected for TWU head, in the GWC meeting for every four year term. And from the regional heads one will be elected for the continental head also for four year term. The regional head will be elected by the heads of its constituent national heads for three year term.

52. The GWC can establish the necessary offices either temporary or permanent, as the case may, for arbitration or for negotiations and some cases as enquiry committees and some other cases for permanent purposes.

53. The establishment of suitable educational institutions will be within the purview of the "United World Educational Organization," which had been established by the TWU for this purpose.

54. The Secretariat will consist of experts committees for budget, planning and administrative matters, who will meet from time to time and deal the matters accordingly.

55. TWU will chalk out plans for the welfare of the whole world, for proper use of the natural resources, and for making use of human resources aptly, keeping in view that *every nation is responsible for the world and the world is responsible for every nation in the world,"*

56. All executive powers are vested in the Director General, he will be of 4 years term, and ineligible for re-election, cannot be a member of any council, tribunal or any committee, for the next one year after the end of his term of the highest position of DG in the Union,

57. The Director General can appoint the Secretary General with the consultation of the GWC and some other councils like Council of Safety and Security, Council of Law and Justice as needed

58. The Secretary General will be for five years term and likely to be extended for another term

59. The World Union will work almost all the year without any vacation, but staff will be on shift system, as it has to watch the whole world without gap at all times, and to safe-guard it

60. The budget and income, levying taxes and making all collections, the security questions will be within the purview of the General World Council, and within the directions of Director General.

61. All legislation is subject to the majority supported decisions only with two thirds majority.

62. No-confidence motion can be moved on any person at the helm including DG and with two thirds majority in the members present. The quorum is also two thirds majority of the total members.

63. There will be twelve supreme Judges, another twelve subordinate supreme judges, another twelve supporting supreme judges selecting six judges from each continent. Their term will be of fifteen years

and then new batch will come, and likely to be extended if his/her services still needed. Their superannuation age is seventy five years if he/she maintains good health.

64. The judges will be promoted from the regional court level, through continental courts. They can put fourth total service about 35 to 40 years in their career.

65. The preamble, the duties and responsibilities, the universal code of conduct and the charter the World Union are to be strictly adhered to both by all citizens and the nations in the world invariably.

66. The law of the World Union supersedes all the other laws and to be strictly followed by one and all (men and nations) without fail, as it is enforceable, and observable and to be obliged.

67. The people and the nations should put an end to all sorts of discriminative practices like caste, creed, race, religion, region, language, skin color, physique, sex or any other such thing.

68. The TWU is empowered to suspend some rights and privileges bestowed on the people or nations in the case of emergency, in a nation or group of nations in view of the safety and security of the world.

69. While enforcing the Union's law the local laws are to be equally respected.

70. Universal education policies are to be enforced invariably.

71. Every individual and nation has the right to move the court of justice at any level, for any legal abuse by any nation at any time, for redress. After due enquiry, the verdict of the court is considered to be final. The Universal Code of Conduct and this charter should be the guidelines for coming to the final conclusion.

72. The capital for the Union can be decided within a year of inception of the Union.

73. The power of amending the charter is subject to two thirds majority of the members present in the GWC meetings, proxy votes may be considered in the meeting depending on the importance of the subject, and the word of the Director General of TWU.

74. This should work with the sole and supreme purpose of promoting and preserving *"The Universal Solidarity and Brotherhood with Mutual Cooperation and Mutual Co-ordination, amongst all People and amidst all Nations of the World."*

75. It should preserve its universal commitment by adapting every nation of the world to be its member without fail. All the continental unions will function in coordination with this Council.

    It empowered to appoint the Secretary-General, and with whose advice establish the Secretariat. And this General World Council will nominate the other principal officials like the secretaries for each council, the jury for the Union's Council of Law and Justice, special military personnel for the Union's The Union's Council for Defense Strategies (CDS) and The Union's Council for Peace, Safety and Security (CPSS).

76. This General World Council is the supreme administrative and supervisory body of the World Union. Almost all matters of the Union will be within its purview, except amendments to the charter. All needed amendments will be made in general meetings of the GWC, annually twice January and July only with due consideration of the majority of the members except on urgent matters like security

aspects. An urgent meeting may be called for on the issues of any calamities natural or man-made. But needed suggestions can be made at any time and any number of times.

77. The budget of the World Union will also be within its purview. The preparation, consideration and approval all will be done annually by considering suggestions and recommendations from the other institutions of the Union, in its annual sessions every December for the upcoming calendar year.

78. The financial commitment lies, on the member-states prorated, depending on their population, and economic status. It is mandatory. At any cost, no member-state should be a defaulter, if so it hampers the safety and security; progress and prosperity, and research and development of the world.

79. Regarding voting- each member-state has one vote for every 100k, or part thereof, population. No veto power for any nation. Any controversy that arises should be addressed amicably with mutual discussions, and should be resolved peacefully. But can be referred to the Council of Law and Justice if need be.

80. The majority in the General World Council general and annual meeting will be two thirds of the member states attended. Postal ballot and proxy allowed for certain issues exempting security, and budgetary issues. The decision of the General World Council is final, but if referred to both the Council of Law and Justice together with the Court of Justice, their recommendations may be taken into consideration.

81. The defaulted member-states has to pay with penalties of adding 50% penalty for each year of default. And hence the member-states are being strongly advised not to be defaulters in any year. Beyond one year default will never arise as all countries are well committed for the world welfare.

82. The General World Council has been authorized to establish its parliament and hold its sessions regularly as per the defined calendar.

Chapter 5. The powers and functions of the councils and institutions of the World Union.

83. Almost all councils and institutions of the World Union should have the single goal to achieve-
    "The Universal Solidarity and brotherhood with Mutual Cooperation and Mutual Co-ordination amongst all people and amidst all nations of the world." So certain things are to be promoted and certain other things are to be curbed by all possible means for accomplishing those goals. In order to establish safety and security, to protect from any terroristic activity, to defend any prevailing war, The Union's Council for Defense Strategies (CDS) is empowered to choose such measures with the consultation of the concerned countries and the people to negotiate and to enter into needed treaty along with the other high officials and councils of the Union.

84. This Council of Defense Strategies and the other councils as well should report to the General World Council, their reports from time to time, for further action. All member states should oblige all decisions that were together taken by the Union's Council for Defense Strategies (CDS) and General World Council in the matters of the safety and security. It is mandatory. Acquiring and stock-piling all

nuclear weaponry and other military equipment should be under the control of this The Union's Council for Defense Strategies (CDS). The Union's Court of Justice has the supreme judiciary power, its decisions and verdicts are final.

85. . Without its clearance no such military equipment should be moved from one country to another. This is the highest safety measure needed for peace of the world. All countries should give an undertaking to this affect.

86. In any voting in order to take right and appropriate decision regarding a conflict, the concerned member-countries should refrain from such voting.

Some Organizational Procedures

The office of the Union's Council for Defense Strategies (CDS) is open and work round the clock, all round the year, to watch the world, with shift batches and should take all the measures for safe-guarding all countries in the world. It alerts the endangering countries for any catastrophes natural or man-made. It will be in the hold of all latest scientific and technical equipment needed. The Council for Peace, Security and Safety will work hand in glove with this CDS.

87. The CDS is empowered to form the necessary offices and appoint officers and can adapt necessary procedures, invite any member-state representatives or persons in the interest of the world safety and security and protect the globe from any calamities natural and man-made.

Chapter 6. The World Union's General Council otherwise called the General World Council (GWC) (contd)

88. The General World Council (GWC) is the supreme authority of the World Union. It works all in all and all other councils work under its administrative and supervisory powers.

89. All countries of the world will unite and form this "the World Union." It is mandatory for every country to be a member of this Union and follow its principles for establishing the welfare world.

90. The member–state is represented by the head of the state or his nominee and can have another associate representative without voting right in all the meetings of the TWU and its subsidiary councils.

91. Except any amendments, all matters may be subject to discussion in the meetings of TWU. The final decisions are subject to voting.

92. The TWU will consider all suggestions and recommendations made by the other councils and bodies, regarding, military affair concerned to safety and security; and for preserving and promoting the main theme of the Union as mentioned in article 28.

93. Each member of TWU will have another permanent representative in the Union for three year term and a new incumbent will be nominated by the respective member-states. Those have no voting rights except in the absence of the main member.

94. The TWU will refer the matters concerned the world safety to the concerned councils, and legal matters to the Council of Law and Justice and the other concerned bodies. But it cannot enforce its individual decisions regarding any conflict between any two distinct countries. It can open consultations with any other concerned council, discuss with Council of Law and Justice and the Court of Justice as well. The verdict of the Court of Justice is final and the concerned countries should invariably follow.

95. When the Council of Law and Justice and the Court of Justice are working on any dispute of any two countries, solely they both try to solve that, if they fail can consult TWU. Then it will also be brought to the general body meeting of the TWU for referendum, and then will it again go to the Council of Law and Justice and Court of Justice for the final verdict. And then it will be final. Then if the two countries concerned do not accept the verdict all the other countries will enforce those countries to accept the justifiable verdict given by the global court. By amicable discussions and by entering peaceful agreements the conflict should be closed.

96. In such cases the Secretary General of TWU will play crucial role in bringing the matter to the notice of all the members of the Union, and enforce the conflicting countries to concede the request of the concerned councils and to end the conflict amicably.

97. The GWC should always be in the concern of the world development following the principle mentioned in §28, And can have open dialogues with all its councils, institutions, and the countries as well from time to time and work incessantly. It can make needed recommendations to all the concerned countries regarding international collaborations and cooperation at all times and should do all the needful in this regard.

98. By having different wings in its office TWU should work in all possible fields concerned namely economic, political, social, humanitarian, philanthropic, scientific, technological, industrial, cultural, and ideologies developments. Besides it should concentrate on both the education at all levels and health to all and all exploitations in the field should be minimized. A global culture should be developed by it.

99. TWU should promote the 'Universal Code of Conduct' both for the whole humanity befitting for the present day and for all the nations in the world. Then the ideological differences will be minimized in the world and the aspired world of peace and tranquility will emerge.

100.TWU should also work in minimizing the discrimination on the basis of cast, creed, race, religion, region, age, gender, language, and ideology. All men and all nations will be treated equally at all times and in all places.

101.While sending recommendations to all other councils and bodies, TWU will take into consideration all suggestions made by them and keep them for open discussions among all members of the Union.

102.TWU should work in all aspects concerned either defense or development strategies with the cooperation of its different wings and also with the cooperation of all countries in the world.

103. After the advent of 'The World Union,' all countries can minimize their defense budget, and can contribute the maximum possible to the Union, and cooperate with it for its smooth and efficient running.

104. 'The World Union' has to run on the contributions made by all members of it, as it works for common good of the world. It is a democratic institution defined as *"by the nations, of the nations and for the nations."*

105. The GWC will prepare the Union budget, and approve its accounts yearly and will make requests to the nations for their contributions in time, as the whole expenditure of the Union lies collectively on the shoulders of the member-states only.

Voting in the meetings of the Union and its bodies.

106. Each member-state will have only one vote. Strength of the vote depends on the population in addition to economic power of the country. Strategy of Mahabub Ul Haq and Amartyasen can be utilized for determining the strength of the vote.

107. Decisions in the meeting will be bound by two thirds majority of the present and voting in the meeting. Two third member presence will for the quorum for the meeting.

108. All member-states should invariably pay the dues by first January every year, if delayed it has to pay with penalty depending on the time of delay. In no circumstances no country may default for more than a year. If so all rights and privileges including the voting right it had been endowed with by the Union will be ceased.

Procedure

109. 'The World Union' will hold half yearly meetings, besides emergency meetings, meetings on the request of the majority of the members, or as it deemed needed in any political, socio economic upheavals.

110. The General World Council will adapt its own procedure electing the president for the session each time and get the business done.

111. The GWC can establish needed bodies to perform various functions of the Union.

Chapter 7. The Council of Defense Strategies (CDS) & The Council Safety and Security (CSS).

112. These are the two important councils of the Union safeguarding the whole world from aggressions, war, terrorism, and civil disturbances besides natural calamities in any nation. They have to preserve and protect peace of the world by all means besides its progress and prosperity.

113. These two bodies consist of member countries having stronger economic excellence, higher industrial growth, higher scientific and technological advancement, and higher population. Namely, the Council of Defense Strategies consists of- for example, United States of America, Russian Federation, Peoples' Republic of China, India, France, United Kingdom, Brazil, South Africa, Australia, Japan, South Korea, South Arabia, Iraq and Iran, Egypt, Northern Ireland and so on.

114. And the Council of Peace, Safety and Security (CPSS) consists of- for example, Canada, Mexico, Argentina, Sweden, Norway, Denmark, the Netherland, Singapore, and Malaysia, Thailand, USA, Russian Federation, Uzbekistan, United Kingdom, Sri Lanka and so on.

115. Each member for these two bodies will be elected for three year term and can be re-elected for the next term.

116. Especially these two bodies have to work hand in glove for global safety, security and peace and submit the yearly proposal for maintaining the Union's army, the three wings infantry, navy and air force besides special army of advanced technology with nuclear weaponry and chemical and biological weaponry, the submarine squad, the intelligence bureau, but with all the aim of progress and development of the world.

117. After TWU's approval, they have to maintain all the needed personnel, and the military force. These two councils are specially empowered to maintain all defense needed personnel around the globe to preserve peace and provide safety and security to all countries in the world.

118. The decisions of these two councils are concerned with global welfare, safety, security and peace, all member-states are bound to oblige inevitably.

119. These two councils after due consultation with the GWC, may take decisions and can enforce them, before that they should follow minimum utilization of human and financial resources and movement of weaponry. And the principle of §28 should be strictly observed as it is the sole aim of the union.

Voting in these two councils

120. There will be fifteen member-states in these councils. Each member-state has one vote to cast. Two thirds majority will be counted for making decisions and enforcing them. In case of conflict, the conflicting nations should abstain from voting, but can participate in the deliberations to project their point of view.

Processes and procedures in these councils

121. All the members and exceptionally their representatives must be present at meeting of these two councils without fail. These councils work round the clock and round the year to watch the world and so shift system for the staff will be maintained with eight hourly duties, to process the information from around the world and to function accordingly with meticulous care and attention.

122. The platform for these councils' meetings may vary according to the need of the situation and occasion, with the needed members, besides all member meetings at the Head Quarters.

123. Any member of the Union can participate in the deliberations of the councils without any voting right, but can express his/her opinion on the issue concerned.

124. The councils can formulate short term body/bodies for solving the situation and enforcing the decisions amicably by all possible means.

125. If any conflict arises anywhere in the world between any two countries or any two groups of countries, these two councils should immediately jump into action to solve the situation by peaceful means and adapt necessary steps of arbitration. From time to time GWC should also be well informed, about the latest situation of the conflicts and seek needed advice as well.

126. Any member-state can bring any conflict/conflicts that arose anywhere in the world, either in their own country or between any other countries of the world, which need to be solved by the Union, as it is beyond their limitations.

127. The GWC with consultation of the concerned bodies will take appropriate action concerned the conflict. Regarding any dispute, it may consider any referendum from the remaining member-states except the conflicting members and in the councils concerned with due discussions and negotiations, may come to the final conclusion, solving the situation. Even the problems having legal aspect involved, consulting the Union's Court of Justice and the Council of Law and Justice and then it should arrive to the final conclusion amicably.

128. Active consultations should be made with all the concerned involving almost all members of the Union as well in getting the solution for the conflict that arose anywhere in the world and positively subside that at any cost peacefully as it involves the global peace and hampers world development. All member-states should also be actively involved in this process.

Chapter 8. Procedure to be adapted in tackling war like situations by GWC, CDS, CPSS

129. In case of civil disturbances in any country, aggression, war, affecting the peace and tranquility of any nation and the world at large immediate action should be taken by the above three councils with the support of all the member-states. If need be emergency meetings will be held at the Head Quarters and at the appropriate places as well to tackle the situation efficiently.

130. These councils will make almost all members-states to involve in the turbulent situation and bring it under control avoiding any untoward activity.

131. These three councils, at the first hand consult with the aggrieved parties hold discussions and negotiate with both the parties and strive hard to pacify the situation. The report of their efforts will be placed before GWC general meeting involving every member.

132. These three councils will lead the situation most peacefully and amicably restricting the usage of armaments and military personnel.

133. All members /representatives of the Union should make themselves available at the Head Quarters at such situations invariably as it is concerned with the global peace, safety and security.

134. All members of the Union should assist in tackling such gross situations by all possible means.

135. After arriving at an amicable agreement, the concerned parties duly sign and confirm it.

136. If not these councils may be constrained to use force, then they should call the parties concerned and get them involved and try for amicable solution as a last resort.

137. In grave situation high military commands of the Union may also be taken into confidence and then final decisions are to be taken and adapted.

138. The Union and these two councils should maintain strong military bases at the strategic points in various countries of the world.

139. All member-states should reduce their own military budgets and contribute maximum possible to the Union to make it stronger. The defense strategies will be worked out soon. Regional-wise and national-wise military bases will also be notified after having the meeting of these councils.

140. The global safety, security, peace and progress and development are the subjects concerned to all nations in the whole of the world and no one should shirk its responsibility. As it is said already as

"Every nation's responsibility is for the world and the world's responsibility is for every nation of the world." Thus "the World Union" will be the savior, servant and master of supreme stature of the entire world.

141. Hence there exists no domination, no inferiority and no superiority amongst the member-states of the union. This principle should be strictly adhered to.

142. All member-states should carry out the decisions of the union without any reservations.

143. All member-states should follow to preserve and protect the sole principle of the Union as mention in Article 28. *"Universal Solidarity and brotherhood with Mutual Cooperation and Mutual Co-ordination, amongst all people and amidst all nations of the world."*

144. These three councils have the authority to direct any member-state to follow the direction given by them invariably for keeping global economy balanced besides safety and security.

145. Any aggrieved member-state should report the Union authorities any threat, aggression by any other member-state for immediate redress.

Chapter 9. Regional distribution of the Union's responsibilities.

146. To preserve and protect and for progress and prosperity of the entire world, the Union's prime goal. Regional offices may be established and outside institutions may be consulted in the opportune and strategic places. And the concerned bodies and the people should be sincere and genuinely work hard in saving the situation. Less serious problems should be solved amicably with these local bodies, if

beyond their limit go to continental unions and then to the General World Council. The power for severe military actions, enforcing the decisions solely lies with GWC and on its direction on CDS and CSS or on the other regional bodies and the government of the concerned nations.

147. Every member-state is friendly state and so should be well treated with all friendliness and all the negotiations will be in very congenial environment.

148. The outcome of all those deliberations should be well informed by the concerned bodies to the TWU or GWC.

Chapter 10. Council for Progress and Prosperity (CPP), Council for Philanthropic and Humanitarian Activities (CPHA), Council for Scientific, Technological and Industrial Development (CSTID), Council for Research and Development (CRD)

149. These four councils work together for the development of the world by developing ties with nations as per the need, the situations and opportunities. They work for the all round development of all nations of the world, matching with the appropriate nations for mutual cooperation and mutual coordination.

150. Also these four councils are responsible for bringing social, economic and political stability in the world and hence, should work with extreme care and plan. Keenly watch the world situations and plan ahead for the world development in all fields along with good life and living, mutual respect between member-states, and respect among people of the world. Protect the world from any economic depressions, famine and catastrophes natural or man-made and should concentrate solely on the world development.

151. They should make the society to progress well and develop fully democratic systems all over the globe in all national and international activities political and social.

Chapter 11. Duties of the other institutions of the Union

152. The all round development of the world should be looked after by the Council of Progress and Prosperity (CPP) with the consultation of the rest of the councils from time to time and chalk out plans and programs and promote the work concerned in all countries of the world. It can develop the necessary bodies when and where needed and get the work done efficiently following the prime motto of the union as given in §28. It should elect its own Chairman, and the council's executive committee will be nominated by the GWC from among the heads/representatives of the member-states.

153. The most social service oriented institution of the Union is Council for Philanthropic and Humanitarian Activities (CPHA), which has to look after the welfare of the world by helping the needed and effected countries due to natural calamities like floods, famine, earth quakes and so on, besides the war-torn countries. Assistance to the poor nations in all possible means should be the prime importance to this council with the consultation of other councils.

154. As the Science and Technology are highly important in the industrial development of the world, this Council for Scientific, Technological and Industrial Development (CSTID) should take the prime concern and responsibility for these aspects with the collaboration of other councils like Council of Research and Development (CRD) etc. All research institutes, universities and educational institutes will be taken under its purview for advancement of science and technology and for research and development and ultimately aim at the industrial growth of the world.

155. Similarly all other councils have well defined commitments, and have to work collaboratively to fulfill the prime motto of § 28.

156. The research and the consequent development has to be looked after by The Council for Research and Development (CRD) and all concerned institutes the world over will be under its purview and it gives guidance to all countries of the world and help for their growth and innovation.

157. All educational institutes in the world should be associated with this sole organization namely The United World Educational Organization (UWEO), which will develop them all in the world perspective. So the whole world is within its purview for educating the masses with broader outlook and minimizing all disparities and differences to build up a harmonious world. It is the universal prestigious organization.

158. For the development of the world and the countries in the world global trade plays important role. And it will be looked after by The Council for Trade, Commerce and Business (CTCB).

159. The world's economic, social and political affairs will be carefully looked after by the Council for Economic, Social and Political Affairs (CESPA), aiming to fulfill § 28 with the collaboration of the other councils. This council will define the universal code of conduct for promoting and maintaining human respect and dignity by all means. The Universal Code Conduct is given in V chapter as given below

Universal code of conduct:

Universal Code of Conduct for the individuals

- ➤ Develop universal solidarity and brotherhood and thus, the unity of the whole humanity
- ➤ Respect religion, every religion, it is a way of life to follow with unity of all religions
- ➤ Hate none but love everyone, love the society, love your country and love the world
- ➤ Do not suppress, oppress or belittle others; honoring others means honoring yourself
- ➤ Be well concerned and benevolent towards the suffering, the aged, the women and children with poise
- ➤ Be contented, with self control; never be angry and be truthful and trustworthy
- ➤ Help yourself, and help others to the best of your ability without anticipating any returns,
- ➤ Develop mutual cooperation, coordination and collaboration
- ➤ No ideology can be coerced, religion and science should be well-synthesized for the life and its development
- ➤ Freedom, liberty and justice should be prime factors of everyone's life, relinquish all prejudices
- ➤ Do not preach precepts without you practicing and serve the humanity by all means
- ➤ Be loyal to your family, to the country and to the world, and be responsible to this world of yours
- ➤ Be righteous and noble, and be pure and pious and have ethical values with honesty
- ➤ Everyone should preserve the nature as best as he can, should not mis-utilize the natural resources
- ➤ Fight not with anyone, but behave amicably, and develop right and rational thinking
- ➤ Develop inner peace and joy by having wisdom and right knowledge, and be virtuous
- ➤ Every individual should work for the welfare of the society
- ➤ Cooperate in finding solutions for all social, economic and political problems of your country and the world as well.
- ➤ No person should infringe the rights of others, what so ever, in any way.

Universal code of conduct for the countries

- ❖ No country should even try to wage a war, attack or aggression on any other country
- ❖ No country should meddle in the domestic affairs of any other country, uninvited. No nation should interfere with either external or internal problems of any other nation without invitation.
- ❖ Every country should strive for peaceful coexistence, with amity and friendship with all other countries
- ❖ Every country should live with other countries with mutual cooperation, mutual coordination
- ❖ Any country can collaborate in research and development with any other country at free will
- ❖ Any country can collaborate with any other country with absolute freedom in scientific, technological, industrial and agricultural developmental activities.
- ❖ No country should cross the borders of any other country illegally
- ❖ No country should obstruct or exploit the natural resources of any other country
- ❖ Every country can maintain its own sovereignty and allow other countries to maintain their own sovereignty
- ❖ Every country should follow strictly democratic principles, and take peoples' referendum whenever needed.
- ❖ No country can use any weaponry, military power on any other country at any time
- ❖ Every country should minimize its defense budget by all means, and support the Union absolutely
- ❖ No country should acquire nuclear, chemical and biological weaponry, and pile up
- ❖ Every country should enter into Nuclear Proliferation Treaty with the Union and strictly adhere to it
- ❖ Each nation is responsible for the world and the world is responsible for every nation of the world.
- ❖ Every country should bind over with this code of conduct inevitably, and follow it strictly.
- ❖ Every country should obey the charter of the World Union
- ❖ Every country should be promptly pay the Unions contributions without fail
- ❖ All countries should cooperate for the establishment of united world, through this Union

- No country should take reins of power of any other country in any means, what so ever may they be except in grave situations with the direction of TWU, then it should be restored as early as possible
- No country should hoard arms, maintain military, and organize any military training camps as the Union is in-charge of safety and security. All military alliances between any two countries are prohibited.
- No nation should maintain suicide squads, human bombs and such training camps either in their own or in any other country.
- The act of spying by all means by nations is strictly prohibited by the Union
- This Union is built up strictly on the principles of democracy, and all member-states should follow the same democratic principles.
- This constitution is strictly republican with powerful judiciary, and on its direction its legislation will work.
- Every country should concentrate on its own development by all means at all times, and cooperate with others also.
- Every nation should strive to built a welfare world society
- For any new concept or interpretation of any existing concept of religion, faith, ideology is to be brought in, or is to be included in this list, the prior approval and acceptance of the World Union is to be taken by the concerned that is mandatory.

This code will help- to fulfill the prime slogan of the "World Union", as

Unite, all nations of the world
Unite, the whole humanity of the world

160. This CESPA will look after the whole of the world humanity for absolute freedom and full liberty without obstructions anywhere in the world. The caste, creed, race, gender, region, religion, language, age should not be influenced the human dignity and stature. This council will take immediate action by itself or through its agencies and watch carefully round the clock all over the world and ascertain the information.

161. The man power is as important as anything else in the world. Man hours both skilled and unskilled are needed for the country and for the world as well and hence to be carefully managed for the development of the world. And hence this separate body The Council for Human Resource Development (CHRD) works in these directions.

162. However best the world development is there, as far as human element is involved, there will be numerous problems, man-made like global conflicts, border disputes and so on. Yet times they cannot solve them by themselves except resolving to war or aggressions. To avoid such things the two important bodies namely-The Council for Law and Justice (CLJ), and The Court of Justice (CJ) will work together and they strive to resolve the conflict in peaceful manner by agreements and negotiations.

163. The Council for Fine Arts and Culture (CFAC) will work together with the collaboration of many other concerned councils, organizations, and the concerned countries.

164. The whole world is depending totally on agriculture and this is to be carefully dealt with by suitable institutes of the union and The Council for Agriculture, Farming and Animal Welfare (CAFAW).

165. For maintaining a healthy and harmonious world health is an important aspect, which will be dealt with, by Council of Human Health and Medical Research Issues (CHMRI), which will consider all medical related issues the world over uniformly.

166. All these councils should work united with mutual cooperation and coordination to achieve the goals of TWU, with mutual understanding and mutual considerations.

167. All the other bodies specially established by the TWU or its institutions should work with the Union solely for fulfilling the motto of article 28, considering its advices and suggestions. These bodies may be established either permanently or temporarily anywhere in the world and in any country of the world for easing the situation and to solve the problems that arose, the problems may be economic, social or political, or any catastrophe natural or man-made that occur.

168. The GWC can empower anyone or anybody for fulfilling the objective that was assigned to it to resolve. It should plan for conventions and conferences country wise and global wise, inviting all the concerned and review the work from time to time and should make further recommendations to the appropriate councils.

169. All these councils can develop the necessary bodies when and where needed and get the work done efficiently following the prime motto of the union as given in §28. It should elect its own Chairmen, and the council's executive committee will be nominated by the GWC from among the heads/representatives of the member-states.

Chapter 12. Composition and function of the councils and the subsidiary bodies.

170. All councils will have twenty five members uniformly nominated by the GWC, and some six co-opted members. From among them one Chairman to be elected who will form his own executive committee, having Vice-Chairman, Secretary, Treasurer, and the rest are to be the members of the committee. They work for three years term. They meet as frequently as needed and work for the development of the world in all possible means and in all dimensions. All its subsidiary bodies will be established by the concerned councils as the case may be. Hence those have to work strictly under the authority of their concerned councils only but cannot work independently.

171. Every year twelve members retire and new members will be infused. The retired members will come into the office of the membership after one year gap. In lieu of each member there will be one representative member.

172. These council together work for the growth and innovation of the world and hence study and prepare schemes and programs with the consultation of the other councils and execute them with the support of its subsidiary bodies.

173. These councils may enter into agreements with other international bodies or to whom so ever it feels necessary and gets them approved by the GWC and then implements the same for the welfare and development of the world.

174. As all member-states are in the advisory position, the GWC can take into consideration the advice and suggestion of any member-state and present it in the general body meetings for further consideration and assigning to the concerned council for implementation after due approval and clearance. The TWU's administrative procedure is to be always followed by all the councils without fail.

175. The GWC should coordinate the works of all councils and their subsidiary bodies very carefully even in the most odd circumstances, with the aim of motto of the union as mentioned in §28 and in the preamble.

176. The GWC should be in the consistent contact with all the councils, and all the countries in the world and ascertain the latest developments in all fields and bring before the general body meetings and assign to the concerned for further action.

177. The problems regarding safety and security and peace of the world, immediate steps are to be taken convening the meetings of the Councils of Safety and Security and Defense Strategies also the Court of Justice and the Council of Law and Justice.

178. All the Councils should work all that within its competence and pass on to the concerned councils and to the GWC as well. And after the approval of the GWC, pass on to each member-states for their opinion and the decisions will be peacefully implemented. If need be the assistance of the specialized bodies will also be taken into consideration.

Voting in these bodies

179. Each council has members constituted by the GWC from the member-states, and each such member-state has one voting member and another associate nonvoting member. No vito is there in any of the councils or in the GWC. In all such meetings for voting two thirds majority will be taken from the members present and two thirds of the members will form the quorum of the meeting.

180. Yet times certain commissions may be appointed to fulfill certain tasks, by any of the councils to ascertain and analyze some information.

181. In the special meetings of any of the council certain member may be invited without any voting but can participate in the deliberations.

182. Without any distinction the GWC can invite any person or institution for needed discussions at all times with a view of harmonious development of the world. They may not have right of vote but can involve in expressing their opinions and views.

Chapter 13. Membership for small and insignificant countries

183. Some of the countries are not the members of UNO like Vatican City, Taiwan. But in the World Union all countries in the world will be member-states mandatorily. They do possess all rights what the other countries possess. Their deliberations will also be considered if found useful.

184. As per the preamble and §28, the Union has to safe guard the interests of each and every inhabitant on the face of the earth and every nation in the world map. Then only the world development can be easily achieved. To this end, the cultural aspects and education, medical and economic growth and all of these countries are to be taken into consideration and assistance is to be provided.

185. More assistance is to be provided by the World Union to the nations lagging behind economically, socially and politically and bring them up along with any advanced country in the world.

186. To achieve harmonious and peaceful world all disparities are to be minimized, all men should develop and their countries should flourish with progress and prosperity for which this 'World Union' has to strive hard.

187. Under UWEO the best educational institutes should be established at all levels in those under-developed countries, perfect medical aid should be provided and should also be developed industrial wise. Consequently economic, social and political development of all countries will take place.

188. To deal with such countries some special bodies should be established, within the administrative purview of the TWU.

189. The TWU should always look out the common good of the people and welfare of the world in all possible dimensions socio, economic and political and humanitarian and make all councils to work in this direction.

190. All member-states shall be divided into six different groups as per their economic stature. Countries of the low economic stature will be well taken care of by or adapted by the higher economic statured countries and help them by providing needed educational, technological and industrial development. The cooperation of the concerned councils may be taken in this regard. In grouping the countries the Human Development Index studied by the Pakistani Economist Mahabub Ul Haq and Nobel Laureate Amartya sen is to be followed for 188 countries in the world. And for the rest of the countries it should be well judged and suitably placed.

191. Besides global safety, security and peace the prime motto is laid in §28, and this should be achieved. And so needed steps for social, economic, industrial, political, cultural and educational progression should be taken in all countries of the world by this TWU.

192. The TWU should take necessary steps for maintaining human dignity and stature with freedom and liberty regardless gender, caste creed, race, religion, region, language, geographical, and skin color and help each individual to grow and innovate in their fields.

193. *As all men born equally,* all human beings should be equally treated at all places, in all countries of the world. All differences, disparities in ideologies should be minimized by developing them by socio, economic and political progress. Modern outlook should be inculcated in all the individuals including

fundamentalists. Thus the countries lagging behind will rise to prominence. All war-torn countries and terror prone states should be dealt with meticulous care.

194. But all countries enlisted as members-states of the Union will be treated equally and needed sovereignty should be provided without affecting their freedom and liberty.

195. When dealing with the troublesome countries the Council for Safety and Security and the Council for Defense Strategies should be well consulted and the military personnel of the Union should be well alerted. The principle lay in §28, and in the preamble should be kept in mind and all aspects like socio, economic and political will also be appropriately considered in these countries.

196. These specific countries should be well involved in maintaining internal peace and security and work with the Union authorities for its developmental process without any obstructions. Then only the world advancement will result in. The Union should accept the facilities provided by such countries without objections.

197. The GWC will administer all matters concerned to the Union; consider all requisitions from its member-states, recommendations given by the other council and council members, opinions expressed by the people having expertise in the matters to be dealt with by the Union and so on. And it directs the concerned councils and individual to work on the specific guidance given by it.

198. The GWC with the cooperation of the concerned continental unions and Union's councils study each and every country's position and economic status and political developments and bring them under the democratic purview for the smooth governance of the country.

Chapter 14. The Court of Justice and the Council of Law and Justice

199. For the maintenance of law and justice and to maintain global peace there are primarily two bodies for the Union namely The Council of Law and Justice and the Union's Court of Justice to tackle all global issues more amicably and agreeably.

200. The Court of Justice has its own statute and all member-states and hence, their representatives are subject to this statute and the court's verdict is final and to be obeyed by all the members inevitably.

201. Before moving the Court of Justice the concerned members may approach the Council of Law and Justice for redress.

202. If the party do not comply with the court verdict then the Council for Peace, Safety and Security also to be considered for further action, like establishing special tribunals to bring an amicable solution basing the court's verdict.

203. Further it will be placed before the General World Council's general body meeting and thus bring before all members of the TWU and the issue will go for referendum. The parties concerned are bound to follow the general polls opinion.

204. Advices from the other councils concerned are mandatory as and when needed.

Chapter 15. The World Union's Secretariat

205. The Secretariat is the prime administrative office of the Union. The secretary-General will be appointed by the General World Council with the recommendations from Council of Peace, Safety and Security and Council of Law and Justice and advices from other councils as per the need. He will be the supreme administrative officer of the TWU. It will have sufficient administrative staff needed for performing various function in the supreme office.

206. The Secretary-General will attend the meetings of all councils, and actively participate in all deliberations and can make suggestions, keeping in view the Preamble. He will report all the proceedings to the GWC.

207. He plays key role in bringing all matters to the concerned councils, and he should give utmost importance on the issues of peace, safety and security, besides world development aspects.

208. He is totally responsible for the Union's activities and need not consider opinions and uninvited suggestion of all others.

209. Each member of the Union is fully responsible to the Secretary- General and the staff of the secretariat, and should not deter their dignity and status and thus facilitate him/them to perform his/their duties perfectly well. Undue influences should not be exerted on the staff of the secretariat at any time.

210. The staff of the secretariat will be appointed by the Secretary- General on the recommendation of the concerned councils and under TWU regulations.

211. The staff thus appointed will be responsible to the Union and accept the preamble and work with high efficiency, integrity and sincerity.

212. All treaties, understandings, agreements the countries made earlier should bring to the notice of the Union, to avoid all future conflicts. As per the preamble, all member-states should work for the welfare of the whole world; high friendly relations should prevail amidst all nations of the world.

213. The agreements any member-state makes with the Union will supersede all the earlier agreements and all conflicts that arise will be resolved basing on this latest agreements with the Union only.

214. For all practical purposes, the Union will consider each and every member country is as of its own territory and treat equally, and looks after its welfare at par with all other countries to fulfill the obligation bestowed on it by the preamble.

215. The Union will protect each member-state from all aggressions, terroristic attacks, from any outside country, civil disturbances of its own by peaceful negotiations and agreements. It will not shirk away from its responsibility even if any severe military action requires, upon the approval of the GWC, after consultation with CDS, CSS.

216. All member-states will have their own sovereign powers, without causing any difficulty to any other country whatsoever may it be.

Chapter 16. Special Provisions

217. In the emergency circumstances a caucus group is to be formed with concerned and important member –states, and Union officials are to resolve the problem that arose, amicably and peacefully. The problem may pertain to global peace or world development concern, or world trade.

Amendments

218. Two thirds of the members of the Union will form the quorum for the meeting of any council, and GWC also. And out of the members present, two thirds of the support will be sufficient to form the majority and any amendment can be passed with this support. As mentioned earlier each member of the Union will have only one vote in these meetings.

219. These amendments will take place in the annual meetings only when general body meetings will be held. In case of any emergency on the requisition of members of the GWC, an emergency meeting may be called for.

220. Secretary-supreme is the final authoritative signatory for ratifying this charter, any further amendments, and treaties and agreements. All these documents will be safely deposited in the HQ of the Union. The copies will also be circulated to all the members of the Union.

IN FAITH WHERE OF the member-states of the Union, the concerned heads of the states, who are indented signatories of the charter, signed this charter in the city of   on

XII.Conclusion

In this volume I tried to elicit more details of the proposed 'the World Union', and discussed about the 'Universal Code of Conduct' for all citizens of the world and also for all nations of the world. The people while following this code can keep his own ideology intact, as this code is just supplement to their own, but not an impediment to theirs. This code is intended for the united world and for the people living in the new world order. Hence their personal aspects will not be hampered, as every nation is a part of the Union. In this world set up man has absolute freedom and liberty, with free will of life and living.

Epilogue

The whole world is rapidly advancing in all possible dimensions, economically, socially, politically, industrially besides having advancements in agriculture and farming. So if one works with collective efforts it will be more expedient, advantageous, and cost-effective, which has been well realized. Hence collective farming became more popular. The long standing idea of united world spread its wings full-fledged in the beginning of the twenty first century and the whole world is making rapid strides in that direction.

All countries are coming together with equal status, and the whole world molded to be one, and all people are also coming closure, some people gain the status of the World Citizenship even. That is the explicit character of this twenty first century. Wonderfully all citizens of the world and all nations of the world will follow the same code of conduct almost minimizing their own ideological differences even.

The universal solidarity and brotherhood and mutual cooperation and mutual coordination triumph to the brim and the world will flourish with peace, progress and prosperity. That is the Golden Period, where all people will be happy and glorious.

Bibliography

1. Borgese, G.A. (1953), Foundations of the World Republic, (The University of Chicago Press, Chicago, 37; Cambridge University Press, London).

2. Ellwood, Robert S., Alles, Gregory D.(1998), *Encyclopedia of World Religions*, (DWJ books LLc, Facts on File, An Imprint of InfoBase Publishing: 132, West 31ˢᵗ Street. New York, NY 10001).
   Copyright@2002,1998, by DWJ Book LLC, http:www.factfile.com.

3. Herndndez, Ramdn, O.P., (1991), The Internationalization of Francisco de Vitoria and Domingo de Soto, Fordham International Law Journal, Vol. 15, 4, Article 4

4. Mohan, R.N. (2013), Universalization of Higher Education for Global Integration: Global Universities. (Amazon, Kindle Edition)

5. ---------., *Mind A Miracle: Man Magnificent*, (New York, Page Publications), 2014.

6. ----------., *Humano Divino*: The Decisive Destiny of the Humanity, (New York, Page Publishing), 2014.

7. Neff, Stephen C. (2012), (Edit), Grotius, Hugo On the Law of War and Peace
   (Cambridge University Press Cambridge, New York, Melbourne, Madrid, Cape Town, Singapore, São Paulo, Delhi, Mexico City)

8. Plato Republic, trans. Benjamin Jowett, Classics Library, (New Delhi, Rupa Publications), 2013.

9. Smith, Adam (1776, fifth ed.2003), *The Wealth of Nations*, (Batam Classic Edition, Bantam Dell, New York.)

10. Sorokin, P.A., *The Reconstruction of Humanity*,(Boston, The Beacon Press),1948.

11. Theodemocracy – the emerging global paradigm – i

Websites visited

i. http://reference.bahai.org/en/

ii. http://www.bahai.us/

iii. Preliminary draft of a world constitution: http://www.worldbeyondborders.org/chicagodraft.htm

iv. (http://berkleycenter.georgetown.edu/quotes/swami-vivekananda-on-the-characteristics-of-universal-religion)

v. Foundations of the world Republic:
   https://archive.org/stream/foundationsofthe033148mbp/foundationsofthe033148mbp_djvu.txt

vi. Barack Obama's Speech to the Muslim World on June 4, 2009
   https://www.youtube.com/watch?v=B_889oBKkNU

vii. Emmanuel Kant, (1795), Perpetual Peace: A Philosophical Sketch
   http://www.constitution.org/kant/perpeace.htm

viii. Alfred Lord Tennyson, http://www.poetryfoundation.org/poem/174629

ix. Joseph Smith Theodemocracy
   https://democracy.missouri.edu/wp-content/uploads/2015/11/Park-CS-Meeting-3-Reading-Mason.pdf
   https://en.wikipedia.org/wiki/Theodemocracy

x. Arabindo Ghose, The Ideal of Human Unity,
   https://archive.org/details/idealofhumanunit033001mbp

The Authors Profile

The author Nava Mohan, Ratnakaram (R.N.Mohan) was born in Alluru, India in 1942. His school and college education was in Narasaraopet, got Masters from Saugar University and doctoral, post-doctoral degrees and Law degree from Vikram University and elected Fellow of National Academy of Sciences of India. He has nearly 40 years of teaching experience as lecturer, reader (D.A.R. College, Nuzvid, India) and professor (Sir CRR College of PG Courses, Eluru). In 1998, the Government of Andhra Pradesh honored him with the Best Teacher Award. He established Sir CRR International Institute of Mathematics in Eluru, India and acted as its Director. He has good track record of mathematical publications.

He is a world acclaim mathematician and visited Japan, France, UK, Brazil, USA, Poland, Australia, PR China and South Korea and lectured in distinct institutions in those countries. He associated with renowned mathematicians the world over.

He wrote many English poems and is writing some interesting books namely 1.The Aesthetic Appreciation of the writings of Rabindranath Tagore (Createspace, 2016), 2. 101 Letters to Barack Obama, 3. The Mind: A Miracle, The Man: Magnificent, (Page Publishing, New York, 2014) 4. My Reminiscences along with my poems, (Kindle edition, Amazon, 2014) 5. Universalization of Higher Education for Global Integration, United World Educational Organization, (Kindle edition, Amazon, 2014), 6. Humano divino: The decisive destiny of the humanity, (Page Publishing, New York, 2014), 7. The Turning Points: in the Lives of the Individuals and in the Histories of the Nations and the World (Page Publications, New York 2015), He spend some years in the United States of

America during2009-2014
Email:mohan420914@gmail;bhanuratnakaram@gmail.com;kavithaflorida@gmail.com.